An Architecture of Complexity

An Architecture of Complexity

LUCIEN KROLL

Translation and Foreword by
Peter Blundell Jones

The MIT Press
Cambridge, Massachusetts

First MIT Press edition, 1987

Original Belgian edition:
Composants — faut-il industrialiser l'architecture?
© éditions SOCOREMA Bruxelles 1983

Translation from French and Foreword
© Peter Blundell Jones 1986

First published 1986

Printed and bound in Great Britain

Library of Congress Cataloging-in-Publication Data

Kroll, Lucien.
  An architecture of complexity.

  Translation of Composants.
  1. Modular coordination (Architecture)
2. Industrialized buildings.   I. Blundell-Jones, Peter.
II. Title.
NA2760.K7613   1986   729   86-10418
ISBN 0-262-11120-9 (h)
ISBN 0-262-61047-7 (p)

CONTENTS

TRANSLATOR'S FOREWORD

For half a century now the myth has persisted that the Modern Movement in architecture was an inevitable consequence of technological progress: historians and critics have written of a 'machine aesthetic', of functional forms, of mechanisation taking command. Yet a close look at many works of the 1920s causes this neat picture to fall apart: often the functional arguments were naive, the forms created with difficulty by stretching traditional techniques, the production runs for 'type' buildings too short for economy. Besides, the model buildings made so familiar by our history books were rare exceptions in a world still dominated by tradition, and only became 'mainstream' with the advantage of hindsight. Clearly there was a gulf between modernist propaganda and the work produced by pioneer modernists; clearly also the modernist image and developments in technology were related in a much more complex and mysterious way than by the direct causal link suggested.

Although the functional and technological arguments had provided a convenient weapon against the persistence of a tradition already stifled by the academies and fragmented by eclecticism, they rebounded against their perpetrators in the post-war period, when taken up as gospel. History was cancelled, Hannes Meyer's programme of 'measuring functions' to produce a finite, determinist architecture was put into operation,[1] mechanisation was finally invited fully to take command, and the CIAM programme for restructuring the planet in neat packages was instituted, almost as a medicinal measure. All that repetitive mass housing which is now so widely condemned was supposed to be good for people; and architects, who seldom thought of living there themselves, declared that people would like it once they had got used to it. By the early 1970s disillusionment had set in: social failures were already evident, technical failures were beginning to make themselves felt.[2] Architects began to regret the scale and naivety of the programme. In subsequent years they attempted to reclaim ground yielded to engineers and technologists in the fever for mechanisation. In a bid to rebuild their self-confidence they declared afresh that architecture was an Art, that they were Artists.

The break with tradition had been a mistake, and applied style and decoration, long repressed though never eliminated, gained a new respectability. Functionalism, now seen as the cause of every ill, was summarily rejected, and architecture no longer had primarily to be useful.[3] Technology, having led architecture in the wrong direction, was now to become the cart to architecture's horse or be forgotten altogether. Architects began self-indulgently to invest in a private language accessible mainly to other architects: the possibility of more public discourse was cynically abandoned. A new elitism grew hand in hand with the new snobbery which accompanied a political swing to the right. A new interest arose in questions of taste which was tacitly paternalist and ignored quite naively all sociological implications.

Yet despite all surface declarations, despite all the new styling and decoration, the ideological changes of the 1950s and '60s had come home to roost. Under the skin of most post-modern or neo-vernacular buildings of the '70s and '80s lies a plan, a disposition of spaces and a plethora of implicit technological assumptions which all belong to the '60s. A lost tradition cannot be recovered overnight or reinvented, even if stylistic trappings can be grafted on. Despite the sometimes pertinent and perceptive criticism of an excessive enthusiasm for the spirit of the age and of attempts to bind history to a single relentless path,[4] great changes have nonetheless taken place both in technology and in society. These make it impossible simply to put the clock back and to pretend that modernism (whatever precisely one means by that word) had never existed. The question of how architecture should relate to technology has indeed never been more pressing, while the question of how the architect should relate to society, to client, user and builder, is one which architects, ostrich-like, continue to ignore. Finding fault with the style of the '50s and '60s the architect of today sees a change of style as the obvious solution. It never strikes him that it might be his role which is wrong, the whole process by which buildings are designed and built that needs changing. Above all he is mistaken in rejecting modernism wholesale on precisely the same naive basis that it was once praised, for unless we fully understand our failures we shall be in danger of repeating them in a new guise.

The name of Le Corbusier was much bandied about in the popular press in the '70s in connection with the countless bad imitations of his *Unité d'habitation*. He was the real villain, they claimed, the man who said that a house was a machine for living in, leading visionary of the brave new world. Yet those who have seen Corbusier's works and read his tracts know that his concerns were far from utilitarian and his connection with later housing failures rather superficial. The magic in his work was due rather to the new image he created, a new form of composition based on the purist aesthetic, finite, abstract, universal and eternal.[5] This has not lost its attraction, indeed it has given rise quite directly to the work of leading architects of our time such as the New York Five and James Stirling. However, it poses a problem that should be central to the critique of modernism, best explained with reference to Pessac, a housing scheme built by Corbusier near Bordeaux in 1926. In a book written in the late '60s Philippe Boudon described revisiting Pessac:[6] the houses had been subjected to numerous conversions by their owners, wide windows had become narrow, flat roofs pitched, colonnaded spaces filled in and decorations added. While these changes positively demonstrated an unforeseen flexibility, they also destroyed the principal architectural qualities of the development. The complete opposition between the architect's vision and the means by which people express the reality of their habitation reflects an underlying political power struggle and throws into question the architect's right to impose an exclusive image, especially on a domestic programme. Few architects today are prepared honestly to face this problem: Lucien Kroll is one.

Kroll has broken important new ground on both political and technological fronts. The two are closely interwoven, even if the latter appears to be the dominant concern of this book. Kroll first achieved international recognition with his medical faculty buildings for Louvain University, built on the outskirts of Brussels in the early '70s. Known already as a pioneer in participation, he received the commission through student intervention in the wake of the '68 student movement. The design was achieved through a complex group process involving clients, future inhabitants, and architects, work being coordinated by means of a three-dimensional model. The outcome was deliberately made unpredictable, complexity was assured by the nature of the process, and Kroll played the part of orchestral conductor, marshalling and directing forces, but without always imposing his own will and choices. He was trying to mimic, artificially and in a short time, the kind of generative process that traditionally gave rise to the cheek-by-jowl mix of buildings in our old towns and villages. This was not in pursuit of a 'picturesque' aesthetic, even if the result might be so called: it was done to produce a real measure of variety and complexity and to avoid the unification which institutionalises.[7]

The medical faculty buildings were constructed systematically on a grid system, described in detail in this book. This aspect of Kroll's work has been ignored by most Anglo-Saxon critics, perhaps because it seemed at odds with the organic appearance. His architecture stands quite at the opposite pole to the high-tech architecture in vogue at present, where all energy is directed towards a technical image, but underlying Kroll's work is an equally keen technological concern. Just as technology has greatly cheapened many other domestic artefacts in relation to an average wage, argues Kroll, so will it inevitably cheapen building, and we cannot afford to ignore the benefits of such economies. The same goes for the use of computers in design, which Kroll also embraces cautiously: one has to resist domination by the tool, bending it instead to one's own purposes. Optimistically, Kroll sees the computer as a means of controlling the complexities which would develop with a more responsive, more participative way of building, providing us with an escape from the repetitiveness, uniformity and autonomy which have plagued large-scale building operations in recent decades.

Kroll's French is expressive and economical, but difficult to translate directly without leaving an impression of franglais. I have therefore reorganised and paraphrased sentences, but without changing the organisation beyond sentence level. The original title, *Composants*, translates literally as 'Components', but this sounds too technical in English, omitting the sense of *composer*, to compose. The suggestion that it be called 'the architecture of complexity' met with Kroll's approval, and he has also checked the translation. I have added a few notes where I felt clarification was necessary.

Peter Blundell Jones   *September 1985*

Notes

1. Among modernist pioneers, Hannes Meyer was consistent and most extreme in his advocacy of a scientifically-based functionalism that was entirely quantitative. See his essay 'Bauen' of 1928, English translation in *Programmes and Manifestoes of 20th century Architecture*, ed. U. Conrads, Lund Humphries.

2. The turning point seems to have been marked in retrospect by the Ronan Point Disaster, 1968. Pruitt-Igoe, the notorious Yamasaki housing scheme in the USA which proved uninhabitable, was demolished in 1972.

3. For these views, see typically leaders in the *Architectural Review*, July 1976 and following.

4. E. H. Gombrich's *In Search of Cultural History* was particularly penetrating, even if the arguments were cheapened and abused in D. Watkin *Morality and Architecture*.

5. The intentions are well described in 'Purism', an essay by Le Corbusier and Ozenfant reprinted in *Modern Artists on Art* ed. L. Herbert, Spectrum Books.

6. See *Lived in Architecture*, P. Boudon, Lund Humphries.

7. For Kroll's own account of the design procedure in detail, see 'The Soft Zone', *Architectural Association Quarterly*, Volume 7 No. 4, pp. 48-59 (1975).

INTRODUCTION: FROM MUD TO COMPONENTS

As much the result of practice as of reflection, this book is perhaps a little difficult, but at least it is short, and I hope will soon be out of date. It was written in protest against the current preoccupations of certain designers and manufacturers, men of power and influence who are preparing, under the pressure of false economy, to devastate architecture yet again. It is in France that these questions seem to be most clearly at issue today, and there also that experimentation with them could lead to a new kind of architecture.

Our aim is not persuasion, but merely to denounce a few absurdities and to underline certain possibilities. In any case, for those who live by the rule book and not by their imagination our line of argument is likely to prove incomprehensible. We are prepared to risk criticising certain practices of the recent past, for such criticism can help define our position and its discomfort. With hindsight perhaps, this is only too easy; but we do after all have the right to prefer Gaudi to Gropius and to say so, even if we have no idea what we would have done ourselves had we lived in their time. In the same way we would like to distinguish clearly between our position and that of other current practitioners, whether we admire their work or feel the need to contradict them. This applies particularly to the present decade with its new sense of freedom which has resulted in the establishment of a new generation of highly creative architects.

Those 'constructional systems' which are derived from 'models', in turn resulting from techniques of heavy prefabrication, are wrongly described as 'open' components, for all too often they fit together only with others of the same type, and are therefore 'open' only within the system. A more responsive components policy would require first the commitment of an industrial manufacturer, then the development and operation of a means of distribution which is competitive and not answerable to the parent company. Only then can the resultant product gain access to the open market; only then can its dimensions and tolerances be coordinated, and only then can it escape the limitations of traditional specifications for materials, conforming instead to new standards of performance and durability. This is surely a long way from the world of mass-produced bungalows and the closed systems we know today.

This book is itself organised industrially: it has a standardised format with specified positions for illustrations. The text was composed directly by the author on a word-processor, allowing a page layout which follows the flow of ideas in a free and responsive manner.

In the course of this essay the reader will meet with a number of themes which include popular tendencies of the moment, industrialisation of architecture, the use of computer techniques in construction and the way these are made available to non-professionals. Sometimes the illustrations reinforce the text, sometimes they inform the reader directly in their own way, so where they fail to speak for themselves they must be understood in relation to the whole.

When I write of tendencies, I mean certain attitudes prevalent in architecture at the moment: the joyous rejection of the Modernist canon, the fertile disorder which accompanies the exploration of a new liberty so achieved, even the cries for discipline from the Old Modernists, which are not really so very different from those of the New Historicists once one has seen through their disguise. We are looking neither for a new orthodoxy nor for a new morality, our aim rather is to destabilise, to remove rigidity, to open up new roads, to retain ambiguity and contradiction: this promises to be more fertile than the adoption of abstract rules which bring with them even more constrictions.

In our time the relationship between architecture and industry is of crucial importance. We bear witness in our text to the obsession of leaders in both fields with consumerism and creature comforts, to their nostalgia for the 1950s when anything could be sold to anyone, and we also show how the naivety of the manufacturers is passed on relentlessly from one generation to the next along with their considerable skills. We go on to demonstrate an attitude towards industrial components which will permit a new kind of decentralisation and a rebirth of the pluralist image. This urgently requires a social context if it is not to be taken over, patronised, or betrayed. We show too how in these conditions an 'industrial way of thinking' seems to us more necessary than the objective study of an engineering office.

Towards the end we describe – from the inside – how we have developed a computing tool, attempting to reduce both its tendency towards automation and its inherent banality, so forcing it to create with all the diversity which it encounters, instead of reducing that diversity. We describe the development of our thinking, our use of terminology, our 'primitive' organisation of the conceptual task. The architects of the last few generations implored industry to take possession of building, and while waiting for this wish to be fulfilled they had imitated by hand the forms that industry would doubtless adopt. But as soon as the industrialists took it up in earnest, they militarised construction in the paleotechnical form of ugly, heavy prefabrication, going on to wreak havoc not only on the physical environment but also in social and psychological realms. They then began to explore new possibilities by creating construction systems. This has led them to attempt to take advantage of a new market in components: will it allow the creation of a new architecture, or is this too to be dismissed as repressive?

This essay sets out to explore the possibility of a real industrialised architecture, a project considered over the years, at times held up, then moved on again by encounters which gave a glimpse of its general relevance, though for a long time it held so little interest for those it should really concern that it seemed to us incommunicable, utopian, impracticable.

Essentially concerned with practice (for one can theorise, but always after the event), this project rests on years of pragmatic thinking, tested directly on industrial architecture (if not always with the willing co-operation of industrialists). It has developed into a sort of intellectual tool, non-theoretical and ready to respond unhesitatingly to a pressing demand. Such a demand seems to be arising at the moment.

The project was initially concerned with society, then with the environment which reflects it, and thus with architecture, construction and industry. Finally it returned to essentials by responding to the active behaviour of the inhabitants. We would like to stress that this is much more than a mere technical question: prefabrication has proved disastrous as an example of how to industrialise building precisely because of its exclusive concern with technique, and for all the use it is now, it would be better banned. A brutal application of the computer to building could be equally problematic. But perhaps we need fear them less when we can ourselves combine these two tools, side-stepping their brutality and using them to discover a new way forward. And, in forcing them to help cope with subjective aspects, we assume that we can avoid the disarticulation which industrial organisation tends to impose upon architecture, with its schizoid juxtapositions of autonomous elements. For at the other end of the scale traditional building permits a continuity of the manual gesture in mud, on wood, on stone, on house, village, landscape . . .

We use the word 'landscape' (*paysage*) in a restricted sense, to denote interior and exterior spaces produced by the many interventions – haphazard, continuous, heterogeneous, instinctive, hidden, convergent, secular, anarchic, in zig-zag, sometimes retrograde, dense, abstruse etc . . . – that men realise in their surroundings. The army, with its discipline and hierarchy, could never generate such a 'landscape' and similar constraints on most new buildings place them also beyond the scope of the term. This is a matter of political ecology rather than objective technique, a point which will be expanded in the course of the book.

1 THE PRESENT SITUATION

'Network' (Réseau): a group of points communicating with one another: the base for lacework with geometric mesh.
Our misfortune: Profit controls the form of developments today, for nobody is made responsible any longer for watching where in the landscape the dragon chooses to rest, to find by this means an appropriate place for settlement.

1. Following the conquest of Morocco, General Lyautey set up a civilian administration and a military garrison for each region. He also delegated an officer of high rank as 'steward for indigenous affairs' who represented the interests of the natives against those of the colonial administration. These officers were respected by both sides. (LK)

Civilian planning

A military attitude to planning is giving way little by little to a civilian attitude, but this can only take place through a series of relaxations, interspersed with relapses into old habits. When planners divided up the infinite diversity of human activities, assigning them to a series of precisely defined zones and reducing them to classifiable types, this was nothing short of colonialism. It involved sending out stewards 'responsible for indigenous affairs' who would listen in a patronising and benevolent way to the wishes of the natives and set everything in order.[1]

As people today propose to develop their own organisation, the old military mentality can only remain deaf to their needs, its tools inadequate. These tools are primarily concerned with economies, with the advantages of technology on a large scale, thus particularly with the provision and removal of fluids: of sewage, water, gas, electricity, electronic communications, vehicles, profits etc. Such 'services' tend to bring with them irrevocable forms of organisation, always hierarchical, with a tree-like structure, never a network. This can only result in 'sewer landscapes' which may be relieved to a greater or lesser degree with embellishments, but remain lacking in real texture. Such rationalisations were probably inevitable a few years ago, but they have prevented a more essential urban order from crystallising out. Such an order can arise out of group intentions, depends on urban instincts about proximities and scale relationships, and can ultimately knit together a whole territory.

This new order depends on new practices, new relationships: it cannot be imposed as a rational procedure. It has to be allowed to arise out of the smallest and humblest initiatives which grow together to form a mosaic, the essential image of the social fabric. This is quite different from the artificial form of the general imposed upon the particular, and it demands tools altogether more refined than those used previously, which were primarily geared to the convenience of technicians. Above all, the new tools must be sympathetic to users.

Social housing in Algiers

New architectural liberation

Suddenly new possibilities are becoming apparent, growing, diversifying, encouraging adventure. The international style, the modern movement, functionalism, even industrialised building are considered passé, and criticised mercilessly. We architects are now escaping from the constraints of the old rules, and celebrating our freedom with a new curiosity in regions long forbidden to us. The vernacular, the antique, the exotic are respectable fields of inquiry once again; there is a new interest in a return to roots, in popular self-expression, sculpture, humour, arts of all kinds, psychology, instinct, local context and so on. We have even tried to imitate the methods of non-architects, whom we used scornfully to ignore. We have also become open to popular pressures instead of limiting ourselves to following the inevitable technology, now recognised for the myth it was. Out of the uncertainty, the diverse experiments and explorations, a new architecture is arising.

Brussels

Geometries

There are (at least) two kinds: the *mechanical* and the *organic*; both are mathematical in so far as they involve the imposition of measure, but behind them lie quite different approaches, for the mechanical dominates while the organic composes.[2] The former imposes its own rules,

2. *This use of the verb* composer *resonates with the original French title of the book,* Composants, *literally 'components' but also 'elements of composition'. (PBJ)*

Zoning

deaf to all other possibilities, while the latter, responsive and sympathetic, takes account of the given conditions.

Making a start
What are the implicit assumptions of the planner? There are at least three possibilities, depending on his political attitude: centralisation, objectification, permeability.

The centralist stance tends to be self-centred, it dominates the sphere of operation, transforming it according to a preconceived image. First the size of the complex is decided, then it is laid out as a single body, in wings or in bays, according to a system of symmetries and axes which is balanced within its own terms to form a self-contained whole. The given length tends to be divided into equal elements, thus whole dominates part. The surrounding landscape is then dressed up and organised with terraces, gardens, connecting spaces, again in conformity with the imposed order. In this way the ordering system which determined the built form gets projected out to take possession of the environment beyond.

The Reichstag, Berlin

Typical of the objectivist stance is a kind of parking mentality, a tendency to arrange things in rows. Such an attitude breeds indifference to the landscape, simply exploiting it, and modifying it purely with a view to one's own convenience. The objectivist does not dress up the landscape in his own image like the centralist: instead he rejects it, detaches himself from it, employing, for example, hard geometries, *pilotis*, and unsympathetic colours and materials which deny any relation with the context. He reduces it to an abstraction or, like the so-called natural parks which are really contrived, transforms it into commodity or spectacle.

He is ruled only by economic considerations, which are essential to his technique and operation, dominated by the profit motive. He calculates according to theoretical units such as the metre or the foot, or he adopts the dimensions arbitrarily set by manufacturers. Without relation to anything local, he chooses ordering systems as incompatible with the landscape as with neighbouring developments. This is an autistic tendency: autonomous elements are set up side by side, disharmonious and unrelated, which could just as well be identical. It also lends

USA

itself ideally to a degree of industrialisation not yet achieved in building, an anticipated Taylorisation.[3]

The third approach, centred on the idea of permeability, involves seeking out and responding to the special conditions of the chosen site. In so doing it should prove possible to discover a basis for formal organisation, to relate the construction process to the immediate locality, to choose an appropriate scale and relevant dimensions. Such an approach can encompass opposites and allow contradictions, but it permits no apathetic indifference. A dimensional module can be chosen which is small enough to respond to the landscape, yet large enough to coordinate the various interventions. The permeable approach remains open to the influence of local history and geography, their development, and the tendencies they seem to suggest. At best it takes root in such considerations, becoming a natural process, almost biology. Ideally it should be able to absorb and take over quite fearlessly any kind of system, tool or calculation. It can even be open to industrial methods and their autonomous processes, taking these as incidental elements in the mosaic of its subjective scheme.

Uzès, France

3. *A reference to Frederick Winslow Taylor, 1856-1915, US inventor and author of* The Principles of Scientific Management *(1911). 'Essentially Taylor suggested that production efficiency in a shop or factory could be greatly enhanced by close observation of the individual worker and elimination of waste time and motion in his operation. Though the Taylor system provoked resentment and opposition from labour when carried to extremes, its value in rationalising production was indisputable and its impact on the development of mass-production techniques immense'* (Encyclopaedia Britannica). *(PBJ)*

Self-analysis

How do we architects see ourselves? This is not a question of corporate identity, but a matter of evaluating the architecture produced: whose game are we playing? Is it our own? that of the capitalists, of charity, of corporate power? Do we serve the priests and bishops, or bow to political or administrative power, or do we turn to local committees, individual inhabitants and their relations? This is surely a question much more likely to influence the form of what is constructed and inhabited than the efforts of architects by themselves.

But as soon as we consider ourselves separately, within the terms of our own discipline, we perceive neither the motives behind our actions and desires nor their effects on the lives of users. 'The fish is the last to discover that he lives in water.' We need an abnormal lucidity if we are to analyse ourselves properly, a healthy scepticism about the comfort of our position, and a passion to lose ourselves in the contemporary human adventure. We must remain coldly critical and not be seduced by power or propaganda, and we must question hypocrisy, so that in the end we can take advantage of the means, and make the most of every opportunity to exploit prevailing conditions as the expressive basis of an architecture. Then we could also no doubt reject those romanticisms which are of such marginal relevance, and the 'business mentality' which is so parochial, in favour of an architecture which simply responds more closely to changing reality.

Rational?

'Everything needs to be rationalised for construction', we decided when under the spell of modernism, and we drew in advance what industrialists might have produced had they chosen to involve themselves with building. Then we forced the craftsman into a narrower role: thousands of identical windows made for Gropius by different craftsmen in a vain, repetitive precision; a motorway proposed by Le Corbusier to cross Paris from west to east; thousands of identical American pre-fabs destined to be destroyed after a mere twenty years. The modernist pioneers got together in Athens to write themselves a charter for architecture and planning, and Le Corbusier rewrote it to purify it more completely of all

Home truths

Why should materials and production processes ruthlessly dictate the form, structure and texture of an object in common everyday use? This madness has produced crude and nasty products which served as barbaric propaganda for a nascent industry. It would be more appropriate to select techniques according to use and to change them if the product gains an unsympathetic image.

Bartning at Siemsstadt, Berlin

reference to tradition, all hesitation, all disorder. He added a subtitle, 'an admonition to right-thinking' . . .

Subjective architecture

Instead of remaining 'objective', some architecture is today becoming more subjective, more responsive to specific incident (place, time, race, tradition, scale, return to roots, climate, recent history, everyday geography etc). This has nothing to do with certain 'Post-Modernists' who are at present asserting themselves. Often this motley crew turn out to be united only in their rejection of modernist forms (for modernism has become the common enemy) and in their efforts to detach themselves aesthetically and technically from everything modernist. Yet only appearances change, while underlying procedures and techniques remain the same. The result is visual and aesthetic boredom. They always conceive their buildings in isolation according to a private vision, then construct them on Taylor's system: their architecture has no connection with a living continuum. Imagine how these buildings will be seen in the future, twenty-five years later.

Militant modernists

It is entertaining now to reflect on the misunderstandings and obstinacies of our modernist years and our naive hymns in praise of industry. Boldly we rejected the obscure and romantic notions of our forefathers in favour of a new kind of hygiene, of rational efficiency, the new enlightenment. We had nothing but contempt for the mysterious, the indefinite, the complex. We then projected onto industry the myths of our new virginity. We tended to ignore the struggle for profits, preferring to believe instead that the industrial order was only there to serve civilisation, and we demanded that construction should express its industrial virtues: long series, rigid joints, new materials, primary colours, identical elements. Fortunately the industrialists of the time did not like it, and nor did their customers.

Some of those who have turned 'post-modern' undoubtedly did so to avoid the mechanistic asceticism of the founding fathers. They share the new desire for freedom, but they assemble their images incoherently. They try to avoid both the hardness of construction demanded by the moderns and the lively banality of popular taste. Fondly imagining themselves founts of wisdom, they take on the guise of historical figures, of classicists, of acrobats etc. Sometimes they appear as madmen or even as neo-modernists (harder still than the original), but always they preach indispensable freedom.

The modernists invented very detailed servicing grids (CIAM, ASCORAL etc), obsessive standards for dwellings, brutal prefabrication systems and a complex administrative mechanism to produce primary elements cheaply. The drawings began to multiply (according to the ideology of standardised types): so they invented the photocopying machine. Variety was next perceived as necessary, so now they have invented the computerised drawing. But will this result perhaps in the same kind of Taylorisation only with prettier images?

We architects announced that we would reform the world through architecture and planning, and when engineers and bureaucrats put a bad caricature of our programme into operation, we were landed with the blame, made all the more vulnerable by the sentimental role we like to play. Thus we are seen as responsible for the new towns and concrete jungles, and our critics are not always wide of the mark. This is a statement of the case, not a criticism, for to sit in judgement 25 years later is all too easy, misunderstandings only too frequent.

Disorder

Having no fondness for disorder, we have prudently ignored it, and have been unable to reckon how necessary it is, how natural or how fertile. In rejecting hypocrisy we have lost ambiguity, complexity, subtlety and contradiction; then we straitjacketed ourselves with crusading

Maybeck, San Francisco

Maredsous, Belgium.

zeal, submitted outselves to the dogma of missionaries, to manicheanism and a naive attitude towards the organsation of work. We recognise only too well now that the idea of an artless small scale capitalism and of free enterprise are mere fairy stories, that in reality we inhabit a world of multi-nationals organised like warring kingdoms. Why should industrialists make beautiful objects if they believe that it is the ugly ones which sell, that it is the cheap and nasty product which earns them a living?

A self-contained aesthetic?
In choosing an unorthodox material through aesthetic preference, we may contribute to the collapse of a region which depends for its livelihood on the production of a more conventional material. This was certainly the case when we abandoned complication and decoration in favour of smooth nudity, destroying a tradition of craft skill. The exploitation and expression of regional traditions is surely among architecture's richest resources. An aesthetic can kill.

The onset of mechanisation
For half a century now engineers – who claim to be neutral, sometimes legitimately – and bureaucrats have pursued their own logic, setting up by degrees a bureaucratic order for the landscape; always constraining spontaneity and collective instincts, and obliterating the past even where its remnants could just as easily have been left. Signs of previous occupation, where preserved, are carefully emptied of their motifs and transformed into cultural objects, expressive of the mercenary concerns of those who organise them.

Constructivists
The modern movement forbade ornament. The facade was reduced to a single material; the door thus looked as if cut by a knife in cardboard. It was legitimated by a constructivist theory which proves nonsensical on re-examination because the forms demanded by construction were in fact concealed; for lintels do not work like cills or thresholds, stops like piers, foundations like cornices, the west like the east, the Italian like the Swede etc. This nudity made some sense in the case of a thick skin of in-situ concrete, but

what a poverty-stricken system! The cold neo-classical styles invalidated the genuine constructive expression of their original models with demonstrative forms that were often useless: columns and facades, for example, became mere curios stuck on to the bearing walls as an afterthought. They were applied purely for the propaganda effect of their form and could just as well have been knocked up in plaster. Corner stones ceased necessarily to support walls, sometimes joints occured in the centre of bosses; in the end they simply painted the plasterwork, as a reminder of what once was. In contrast followers of the Gothic and sometimes of the Neo-Gothic continued to detail their stonework pragmatically with returns, drips and pinnacles in a great variety of profiles and assemblages – except on those occasions when they bolted their stonework onto an iron skeleton.

There is no essential difference between the industrial aesthetic and operetta classicism, for when such architectures are produced coldly they can easily change appearance. We must not manufacture towns but let them arise by themselves.

Operetta stories

Blaming the modern, then copying the past – this is obviously puerile. This 'past' taken in any case out of context is reduced to decor, isolated form, without real meaning and without evolution: in the face of it we became mere tourists, spectators. To be modern is perhaps just to visit without involvement, to take cultures in bulk; does one buy them perhaps in the hope of disguising oneself – as a kind of game? And to be contemporary, is it perhaps just to live in the present, pursuing some chosen style of life? This does not require complicity with the powers that be, merely some sympathy with one's contemporaries, with other movements, parallel tendencies.

We should be suspicious of nostalgic admiration for beautifully organized spaces conceived at a time which has nothing in common with our era, particularly when

Universal Studios, Hollywood

Brno.

Despite all the declarations about honest construction, these forms blankly refuse to tell us how they were assembled by their builders: even the slightest trace of the human hand is removed. However the brickwork eventually reappears as the abstract render falls off, and an unacknowledged part of the building's life is revealed once more.

expressed by those who reject the vulgarities of the present despite an analysis of contemporary desires and their effects which may be intelligent but also sentimental.

This periodic fascination with ancient forms is strange, when they are so unrelated to our own customs and so remote in time. We must not confuse eclecticism with ecumenism (the one borrows, the other exchanges), nor should we confuse Marie-Antoinette with Les Petites Soeurs de Foucault. It is all a question of power, of not confusing colonialism with ecologies. Since the Italian Renaissance the new urban class had joyfully destroyed local ecologies through attempting to impose upon them – with some ingenuity – a vocabulary of exotic forms quite alien to both place and time. And every time a new power wished to legitimate itself, it fed its propaganda machine with these esoterica.

Hollywood, not the architectural academies

Like thousands of tourists I innocently visited Universal Studios at Hollywood: it is here that one sees the future of artificial landscape, much more than in architectural schools and professional circles, for Hollywood already has a hold on the housing industry.

Hollywood is nothing but a factory for public spectacle, and architects are gently moving in the same direction. Hollywood can remain unconcerned with the moral implications of its architecture since its monuments are so ephemeral (as certain prefabricators sincerely wanted their products to be, around 1960). The set is not a large item in a film budget; while architectural budgets tend to contract to a level of sheer mechanical usage (the convenience gained in the use of the crane and mechanised shuttering has proved more determining than that of future inhabitants). In Hollywood they have only to transmit a precise and credible image determined by the scenario, and they are invited to sacrifice everything to it – the contemporary scene, the language, the cultural context – since in the story all belong to the world of the scenario. In the same way some architects only aspire to one quality – saleability. Without any corporate tradition, Hollywood unhesitatingly uses every technical and financial means available. In comparison, architects lag behind: still obsessed with truth to construction (though this is often skin deep or nostalgically out of step with contemporary materials) they find themselves unable to construct things 'dishonestly'. They even rejected reinforced concrete at the beginning: this 'paste-like' material which flows into moulds.

East Berlin.

Disneyland

Architects are searching for fresh convictions, for hard logic has lost much of its lustre with the end of the 'Modern Movement'. Now we have some who pose as Roman comic-strip characters. But apart from the skin what have they managed to change – with all the hymns to industry and in praise of planning techniques, which were expected to produce a definitive order in the landscape?

Infantile architecture

At quite the opposite pole to the complexity of

© WALT DISNEY PRODUCTIONS

the Baroque are two regressive tendencies evident today: the industrial toy, and the fairy story. The first draws on the utopians of the eighteenth century, echoing their bold abstract forms. The primary forms and colours of geometrical architecture tend more and more towards great glossy toys, lacquered, artificial. Any complexity comes only from juxtapositions or interlocking of elements made crudely obvious. Other architectures imitate Disneyland directly with its false legends and its mechanised characters, contributing to a fifty-year-old tradition of Disney architecture which becomes more and more determinedly childish. We have watched the sets of Walt Disney (a great architect) as they became more and more confident and elaborate: these are to architecture as the Club Méditerranée is to real life – the artificial simplicity of a fantasy world.

My Taylor is rich
The division of work is not necessarily a bad thing, nor is it necessarily bad to study the way work is done (even if the first clock-watchers were thrown into the Thames): nor is it necessarily bad to organise work intelligently – indeed efficiency demands it. Taylor's methodology went considerably further: he prevented the possibility of the task organising itself and developing a friendly relationship with the neighbouring task without the intervention of central office. It is a question of power, as by this means work could be subordinated, to the machine and to profit. And at that time, machines were not designed to be user-friendly.

Mechanics
There is an obvious analogy between the world of work and the world of architecture and

Taylor as architect?

While conception has always been partly a matter of automatic animal behaviour and partly of self-consciousness about one's actions, it evolves by revolutions, by sudden leaps and intermediate stages. Without subscribing to the myth of the noble savage (who is supposed to bring knowledge to perfection by successive steps without suppression, developing a stable technique) we can chart the effects of three massive revolutions: the Renaissance, the *Encyclopédie* and Industrialisation. The Renaissance abandoned evidence locally rooted in time and place in favour of borrowing antique exotica and generating utopias. The Encyclopaedia calmly recorded the state of knowledge and technique, believing that these could be held exhaustively in a commercial medium of communication merely through drawings and text – but what do we really know of everyday culture through looking in such manuals? What could not be registered rationally had to be left out (and collective instincts scarcely lend themselves to a card index).

It only *seems* that Taylor concentrated on the production of objects (and what if they had listened to Henry Thoreau?) His military method expressed the aspirations of his time regarding all human action: a latent wish for reification and domination over beliefs and instincts (non-Western cultures paid dear for this violence). Taylor militarized even the army, and also, curiously, the church. But above all he concentrated on administration: bureaucracy is power abandoned to the tool without leaving any room for political creativity.

Architecture too was unable to defend itself. It became ashamed of collective spontaneity: of streets, markets, populism, bad taste, unself-consciousness, of decor, mixture, ambiguity. Without knowing how, we architects became victims, we embarked on this mechanisation and expressed it in metaphors, in commands verging on the criminal, in absurdly overscaled constructions. But we were no more to blame than those ethnologists who conserved for themselves a park of noble savages merely to observe them secretly, or those graphic designers who suppressed capital letters (noble characters once cut in stone) and made texts unreadable through homogeneity of cursives, or those geographers who saw the ladscape as a possible battlefield (and exiled Elysée Reclus[4]) or those psychologists who tickled the unconscious to make people buy things, or many others.

Before attacking industry, we should surely distinguish between the intelligent organisation of group work (which has always existed and which no tool invalidates) and the reinforcement of power which results from organised work. In its brutality at the beginning of the century, Taylorism produced only tools (machines, clocks

planning. In old towns, for example, and even up to the present day in certain areas, activities become specialised. Markets develop according to their own zoning rules, the result of decisions which were shared if not unanimous, remaining also at a modest scale. The novelty of the Modern Movement (soon unacceptable because it operated at such a gigantic scale), and of eighteenth-century utopias, was to create anew out of a vacuum (no local history or geography, no tradition). They destroyed or ignored the context, creating spaces for habitation demonstrably based on purely mechanistic criteria. Nothing left to chance, no disorder, no provision for intervention by inhabitants: technical specialists for everything, complete concentration on the object. When the specialists were artists of high calibre working in the guise of engineers (as in the case of Pierre Chareau with his living-machine in glass – or that of Charles Eames) the resulting poetry was extraordinary and delicate. However, when the specialist became a bureaucrat and worked in a mediocre way, the result was as insufferable as it was inevitable. The machine was launched on its course, Taylor made it cybernetic; it devastated landscapes with a terrible inevitability, the same inevitability that Louis Renault tried unsuccessfully to resist in his factory at the turn of the century. An effective opposition might have developed through structuring production processes in quite a different way, but this was no more straightforward in architecture then than it was to Louis Renault. These days it is beginning to appear here and there.

4. Anarchist French geographer and opponent of Humboldt and Vidal de la Blache. (PBJ)

For several generations of modernists eclecticism and popular decoration were seen as a vice; today it is not so easy to understand why. No doubt it was necessary to live through a phase of austere certainty, to repress historical and regional subtleties, as did those conquering armies which built empires sincerely believing in their duty to spread civilisation, regarding local religions and cultures as objects and curiosities to be collected, never as sacraments. They took the same attitude whether they were in Africa or Asia, and it applied equally at home where they repressed regional variations in language, work, clothes and popular arts.

and methods) but these certainly were not there to encourage self-realisation.

Spontaneity and discipline produce very different ways of working and different arrangements of space and time. Sometimes these result in quite different products even when starting with identical knowledge and techniques. This is not a question of the pious opposition between craftsman and factory, between mason and machine: such imagery neutralises the radical distinction and encourages the belief that spontaneity lies in the dream, in utopia, in the literary world. Finally it achieves the reverse of its original intention: for industrial power, more realistic and in good heart, just faces the hard realities more resolutely.

2 INDUSTRY

Industrial romanticism
The architects of the Modern Movement certainly believed in a real logic of construction, but it is often difficult to disentangle from their appetite for abstract art. Their social attitudes too were by no means clear, except in particularly extreme or brutal cases.

Industrial repetition.

When Le Corbusier dreamed of new cathedrals and wrote so admiringly about American grain silos, he was certainly seduced by the drama of white cylinders in the sunlight on a heroic scale, but those monuments also spelled ruin to the small farmer, who was forced into a servile role, while power became more and more concentrated in great blind institutions. Ultimately it led to the devastation of farmland in the Mid-West where wind and soil erosion combined to produce the Dust-Bowl. When Le Corbusier later allowed himself to be seduced momentarily by Mussolini's Fascism, he was driven by the hope of finding the kind of concentrated power necessary to realise his dream of housing modern society, a vision already conceived at a scale of 25 million units for his client Voisin, a car manufacturer. Such power could also provide the means of halting the spread of sprawling suburbia, with its spontaneity, its cultural vulgarity, its fertile disorder. Thus the Modern Movement was by no means independent of its political context.

Robert Maillart

Jean Prouvé devised ingenious ways of folding metal and created 'machines for living-in' which were both straightforward and poetic. Others preferred to design falsely 'in the manner of . . .' and abandoned the discipline and claims of technique in favour of a purely sculptural intent, producing an abstract architecture deliberately detached from the place, its history, and any cultural roots or memories it might contain. Some even came to compare the bridges of Robert Maillart with paintings by Mondrian or sculpture by Van Tongerloo, suspecting them to have been created like works of art, abstract, utopian, rather than in response to use and locality.

Diversification versus centralisation

Two logics? The natural (*sauvage*) and the military. The architectural instinct is universal, timeless, innocent: at some periods and places it is allowed to act according to its own nature – in villages, shanty-towns, temporary structures, dreams, novel situations.

To organise people into an effective team does

not necessarily involve following a military model, nor does geography presuppose a military outlook. But these are the means which power uses, amplifies, and diverts from their natural course. Self-induced Taylorism? What is the difference between an effective pluralist organisation and bureaucracy?[1] Where lies the frontier? And when industrial power lets its workers organise themselves a little, is this not just a crafty move, just a way of letting the immigrant worker sweat for himself? Or is it the first step in the relaxation of discipline, leading towards an industry which is both organic and efficient? Could the amelioration of the work space simply be the carrot? What sort of space results, is it genuine or are there ulterior motives?

Economists and psychologists hold conflicting views about the machine: it is sometimes supposed to be destructive of the worker's identity, sometimes constructive; it is supposed to eliminate jobs but it also creates them. Surely architects too have a right to cling to their illusions and to create in turn their personal superstitions based on their views of industry.

We should encourage workers in their desire for involvement, let them create their own organisation using the most modern tools, and then watch how it develops. The relationships and spaces which emerge will differ markedly from those imposed by 'experts'. Housing should be subject to the same kind of experiment with reality: the result will certainly differ both in form and in detail from that produced by the usual paternal institutions.

Industrial architecture?

But why turn to industry when we prefer the craftsman? And where do we stand in relation to industrialised construction? Was not the first industrialist merely a well-meaning individual who was trying to distribute the good things in life more widely through quicker and cheaper production? And architecture? Has it not always provided an image for someone: the bishop perhaps, or the colonialist, the rich farmer, Robinson Crusoe, the restaurant chain? It has expressed the social organisation of a village, propped up an insecure government, reassured the *nouveau riche*, at times drawn attention to the architect himself: today it serves the in-

1. *In the original, 'Bureau des Methodes', which is stronger. Kroll explains: 'In a car factory there is a large team which studies the prototype and draws out all the parts. These are then related to the factory machines, production processes, and every operation carried out by the manual worker. This is the Bureau des Methodes, all pervasive: nothing can escape'. (PBJ)*

Glienicke

Schinkel
Around 1825 Prince Karl of Prussia invited his friend, the Tsar of Russia, to stay with him at his summer palace at Glienicke, near Berlin. To honour his guest the prince asked his architect, Karl Friedrich Schinkel, to construct

two buildings in the park. One was a church in red brick where the Tsar could retreat for quiet prayer, the other a traditional Russian izba, a log cabin where he would reside during his visit. Naturally Schinkel chose to adopt a slavic style before any consideration of place or period, in deference to his Russian client. In the palace itself and its ancillary buildings he had already employed a number of styles: classical, romanesque or gothic according to the styles of architectural and sculptural works to be exhibited within. Schinkel's genius is threefold: first, his ability to resolve conflicts and compose his varied vocabulary throughout the park, so that one only discovers each new style as one departs from the last; second, to have made such perfect gems of architecture; third, to have devised them so that they grow old equally elegantly.

dustrialist or the bureaucrat. Until quite recently architecture was rooted in its own history, in mythology, in superstition, in the local landscape; but it has been torn away limb by limb and thrown into a deliberately abstract realm: it became possible therefore to mechanise it in a few stages. Gradually the architectural image was separated from its rightful place and time as architects took on a series of alien roles: first they became Greek herdsmen or legionnaires, decorating their capitals with exotic vegetation, later they played the mathematician, abstract and placeless. Finally they appeared as constructors of family containers stranded between roads and services. Recently, however, all this mental energy and the calculations it produced have been diverted: we should now reapply it to our context, convert it into an instrument which operates on whole subjective networks rather than on isolated elements, abandoning once and for all the idea of an autonomous mechanical system.

Industry depends on selling

'There is a way of looking at the industrialisation of building which yields quite a different image from that cast by architects in the last half century. Under this view it takes its inspiration from the development of other branches of industry and functions quite coldly as the tool of profit, unconcerned with public service or spiritual responsibility. First calculate how to arouse the sympathy of the majority then flatter them until the sale is completed.' Such is the technique of selling. We have yet to see a really profound study in the realm of dwelling and urban planning which is conducted according to this point of view. Let us imagine the nature of this study: it should be *global in scope*, active, neutral, profound, amoral and apolitical, for the seller's aim is to propose models which fit a pattern of consumption – that is, he wants to sell a service, not an isolated product.

It should be *active* because it needs to invent models and test them. *Neutral* because it should show no bias towards any particular party, success being the only goal. *Profound*, because it should go beyond immediate reactions and probe the secret desires and frustrations of the head of the family, in order to understand his self-image and fit the product to it. *Amoral*, because it is not a question of education but of seduction; and *apolitical* because no social vision should be allowed to compete with profit, the sole motive. Lastly, it should concern itself with *groups*, because the built environment is not the product of isolated individuals. A good example of such an approach is the way they researched the

Apart from the power of his genius, what differentiates Schinkel's deviations from Disneyland, the 'Belgique Joyeuse' exhibition, African villages reconstructed for tourists, our own reconstruction of period buildings, or the last government palaces in classical style built around 1950 in Washington? Yet for all their ambiguities these deviations are surely more fertile than the miserable honesty of '50s prefabrication.

'Belgique Joyeuse' Exhibition, Brussels 1958

Such houses are very mechanised, but in a discreet way, for a traditional appearance reassures and sells well: it confirms social status and eliminates contemporary vulgarity. They are equipped with every kind of distraction and creature comfort to persuade you of the benefits available today: the moral comfort of effortless waste disposal for example, and of engineered social relations which eliminate personal problems and minimise disputes with neighbours. This sanitised version of happy urbanity is commercial since it sells reliably.

Village from the Sudan, Paris 1931, a colonial exhibition

What industry really wants is comfortably to repeat the same model without worrying about going upstream or downstream: no problems of history or cultural context, simply selling. Today factories are closing, tools are left to rust, and this has its advantages, for it helps make industrialists think more about context, about other ideas, other methods, expression and variety. Will this prove to be a turning point, a chance to change the form of objects and buildings, to abandon construction systems in favour of a components policy?

2. Kroll is thinking particularly of advertising on French television, which is nationalised but also commercially supported: why pay taxes for television and then have to watch these adverts for useless things, never for bricks or bread or other essentials? (PBJ)

consumer in order to echo his self-image in the design of the modern car, disregarding its monstrous relationship with the city. 'At last we have discovered the noise that a car door should make when it closes', said the highly paid specialists at General Motors who conducted research into motivation. What would they say about the house? The result would be neighbourhoods where dwellings were sold with club membership and prefabricated friends included, according to that deadly formula for a ghetto which the Americans innocently call a 'condominium', where the old live alongside the old, the poor with the poor and so on.

Anti-industry?

The craftsman is flexible, decentralised, ecological, he works on a small scale, but he is being smothered. His products are too expensive, he has to work too fast to keep himself solvent, and he expends considerable effort on mindless drudgery which a machine could do: often he loses in the financial struggle. Against him is hard industry: precise, intelligent, and crafty. It does not make pacts, it simply colonises. It only involves itself in cultural issues to exploit them for increased sales, never for the sake of their expression. 'Ugliness sells badly', ran a slogan, more of a whim than a concern for moral purity (why so much effort to improve sales of cigarettes or gadgets? – publicity material and the industrial aesthetic are concentrated mainly on superfluous products)[2]

Industrial and financial power is born of a military outlook, for what is good for General Motors is also good for the Americas. The industrial product has its own self-contained logic, the only kind of compatibility it knows is mechanical compatibility, it colonises. An architect may be more responsible and more sensitive than the others but what can he do when faced with this arsenal? For a long time now we have sought out exceptional conditions and tried to find the most open-minded industrialists, but without much success. Perhaps the current crises will bring more awareness?

At the same time industry is production intelligently organised, it works at the scale of large teams, handles vast quantities, and can afford to invest in research, equipment, and preparation for a future market. However, Jean Prouvé, industrial romantic, believed in it, associated himself with it, but soon found himself hounded out of his own factory: we should remember that budgets for research in industrial design tend to be less generous than those devoted to wining and dining customers and providing other such 'softeners'. The enforcement of order may be necessary, but do we need colonels? Until now the building industry, by means of its materials and elements, has imposed a contagious image of its own logic of production. It has decisively dominated the landscape, which it has seen only as a base on which to park the objects to be sold, or as a grid of roads and services. It never showed real empathy for or took adequate account of the local network or its history. Some architects are happy with this state of affairs, but not all. Most of us do not feel moved by industrial buildings except when they are deserted, inoffensive; when they become industrial archaeology.

One can refuse to get involved with industry, one can fight it, but one cannot ignore it. It is in direct reaction against industry that fringe tendencies arise – the nostalgic return to stone walling and paving, the old village style, a rustic veneer; and such moves have a certain logic. One can also try to divert industry from its present course: to do so it is necessary to get involved with it, to propose alternative strategies, to be cunning, to exploit mis-

understandings, to attempt piracy, pushing things to the limit to see what can be achieved. This is no fairy story. It can only work once and only in the right circumstances. A man of exceptional vision, a subtle balance of forces, or a fear of commercial failure may precipitate it just once.

Social housing

The door
The entrance is the most sensitive place in a dwelling: it gives some idea of the identity of the inhabitant and of whether he wants you to know about him or not. Not so long ago the window looking on to the street would display a vase, a plant set between glass and curtain, or a statue facing outwards. Even the hem of the curtain was turned inward, the best side being reserved for the street. Front doors had attention lavished upon them, protected by a welcoming porch. The letter box was celebrated, the door knocker a piece of craftsmanship: this is after all the frontier of tactile contact between the outside world and the family. Nothing was abstract, nothing done in a mean or contemptuous way. What has happened to this constructive display of ethnological expression? It is notably absent in the basic modern door with its miserable letter flap in sheet metal and industrial bell-push. Today it is a relief even to see the scrap of sticking plaster which a doctor has stuck under his bell to inform his patients of changes in his surgery hours!

The limitations of heavy prefabrication

When one examines present systems of construction, one finds a pair of contradictory attitudes. On one side there is admiration for technical know-how. This concerns the organisation of tools and workspace, of transport, of assembly sequences and time schedules, also the precise physical and chemical designation of the product.

In contrast with this admiration one finds dismay about the brutality of design, and the puerile architecture which results, impoverished and eroded by the inflexible systems; also disappointment that such concentration on technique achieves so little and remains relatively expensive. How did this come about? Concrete systems are the result of heavy prefabrication, which uses a clumsy method to achieve a very basic enclosure: a mould is constructed in a factory and a wall element is then formed which can be dropped into position precisely by crane. The panel is made as large as possible, with thermal insulation included. It also has to be made watertight: an integral projection gives horizontal protection, a decompression slot and a flashing provide it in the vertical plane, though not very reliably. This was the system developed initially and it has not changed essentially. Around 1960 I asked Camus, the engineer who set up the first construction systems of this kind, what they were doing about the poor quality of the results: the cold bridges,

28

mould growth, lack of acoustic isolation and opening joints. I found his obstinacy and complacent repetition of the same answer incomprehensible: 'We are too busy keeping up with production, there is no time for improvements'.

Perhaps these early models for a new architecture were justifiable in 1950 but they have set the pattern for all prefabricated systems since, excepting certain heroic and sometimes expensive attempts to create a prefabricated classical facade with columns and infill, and various cladding systems. It is always the same joints that fail, the same elements that repeat endlessly the same relentless rhythm, resulting in the same alienation. Architects meekly chose the colours, and sometimes drew the general layout, and were well paid for their pains.

But if the organisation can sometimes be impressive, the use of the product and its distribution through limited and essentially private channels prevents any real industrialisation. If industrial thresholds were achieved, if there were no race by manufacturers to gain the monopoly on production of every element in a building, we would have a much broader range of products to choose from and consequently more opportunity to coordinate them.

Another programme
In opposition to these mechanisations (or alongside them?) we propose the construction of a habitable landscape as part of popular culture, achieved through the participation of inhabitants, with a variety reflecting their wishes. We aim to produce a stimulating urban texture, a network growing out of the existing place and local history Little by little the various means must be polarised towards these ends, and we must cease to think in terms of objects, but instead of elements, assemblies and sequences.

Diversity

Diversity encourages creativity, while repetition anaesthetises it. Often architecture is too homogeneous, sometimes because the type is simply repeated, sometimes because of a self-centred desire to see buildings apart from their context, sometimes because of an exaggerated aesthetic commitment which tends to a precious 'architects' architecture. But whatever the cause, such homogeneity makes it difficult for the users to add anything of their own, and we lose that rich resource of popular creativity which can transform a space into a place and give it life.

New housing developments thus tend to be dull, unsurprising, lifeless, even on those rare occasions when they are well designed. This should remind us that it is inhabitants who really create the city and not planners.

If we were able to obtain the space and the means to allow the inhabitants to organise their own buildings, they would by their own efforts generate both the diversity and the close relation to the fabric which is lacking: that has always been the case. However, with the limited and prescribed conditions under which we work today it is very difficult to achieve such ends. The organisation of large scale construction and the specialisation of trades and tools are supposed to be economy factors, yet often the very centralisation process which made them possible brings its own enormous administrative and commercial costs. For example, what is the real cost per square metre of 'social housing' when one includes the salaries of the housing officers, bureaucrats, ministers, statisticians, accountants, merchants, of writers and enforcers of rules and regulations? How would this compare with the same square metre self-built and self-managed?

How could one combine the advantages of organisation and spontaneity? Through real or simulated participation by inhabitants, and through our efforts to exploit the variety suggested by the place and time, we are able to produce a diversity which we push as far as the circumstances will permit. If the initial inhabitants remain that is fine, but all too often they are prevented by accident, by difficulties or adverse circumstances from doing so. However, the diversity itself has a value, even if artificially induced. It denies the possibility of a finite aesthetic and it encourages extension through the activities of the inhabitants, by additions which may be almost imperceptible at first, but which tend to become more and more marked. It is obvious that the redecoration of a single door in a uniform line of houses by the occupant is a stark political gesture requiring exceptional courage, but if everything is diverse and varied rather than uniform, then timid interventions can gently be made which encourage others of a bolder nature. A process of accretion starts, which grows like a biological organism.

An organic architecture?
When a designer sees his work as part of a continuous context with which it should interact; when he takes into account what went before and what might follow; and when his artistic and technical arsenal serves only to help bring about this product of immediate circumstances, it results more in a 'subject' than an 'object' – in an organic architecture.

But if on the other hand he acts in an isolated way, exploiting the circumstances in favour of his personal product, the result is a technical or artistic object (sometimes autistic). This polarity is a little stark: reality is always more fluid.

3 INDUSTRIAL ARCHITECTURE WITHOUT INDUSTRIALISTS

Our approach to industry
Our own approach to industrial construction has been irrational and, moreover, moral: yes to industry if it produces an acceptable architecture, no if it proposes an image incompatible with or destroys the social and cultural context. It took us a long time to find industrialists sympathetic to this point of view, for most seem quite unaware of the difference between their mechanised production of industrial floorspace and the essential quality of habitation.

We have always opposed the alarming spread of heavy prefabricated concrete systems and their tendency autistically to dominate areas swept clean of all historical reference, but we have persisted in our belief nonetheless that industrial know-how could one day provide the means for an organic architecture.

First of all industry would have to renounce its domination of its built world, so that architecture can become culturally neutral in its relation with modern materials. This would allow it to abandon the self-referential industrial image in favour of a more sympathetic one. It would also allow a distinction to be made between the form which an intelligent organisation of work produces spontaneously, expressing an inherent complexity, and that born of cultural paralysis, with its rigid alignments, its identical elements, its complicity with Taylor's system which splinters work into unrelated fragments.

Anodised aluminium doesn't automatically mean luxury offices and cut lawns: one can imagine it hidden amongst other more popular materials and see it given by contrast quite a different image from that one had assumed.

Industrial power has remained indifferent to

such views, being little interested in the implications of its products as long as they sold well. All our approaches to industrialists thus proved fruitless. But as early as 1952 we put up a prefabricated exhibition pavilion using interchangeable timber elements: badly organised by the client, it ended up in the serving of writs.

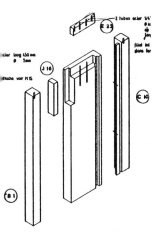

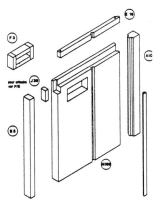

Prefabrication Project 1B 1966-68

This project involved a very small firm in Namur with a large vibrating table, equipment to handle elements in concrete and terrazzo, and a programme of two buildings a month as required. We had observed their difficulties: either they repeated the same model while their clients were demanding something different, or they exhausted themselves in devising moulds which could only be used once.

We proposed that they should rebuild their mould with sliding sides fixable in a large number of positions, that they should choose profiles according to their position in the assembly sequence and in relation to beams, columns, and lintels, and that they should take account of the thickness of the neighbouring panel (add on a thickness, take one off, or precisely to the module). We also suggested that they should leave recesses at the top or side to accept partitions or beams. As each variation is multiplied by the other, a great number of different panel types could be produced by the same tool. We remained undecided, in that period of transition, whether to base the system on the foot, on 10 centimetres, or on a rounded-up version of the Módulor to get the maximum complexity. The assembly of walls and floors was orthodox, the concrete light with built-in insulation.

Nothing came of it: before anything could be achieved the owner-manager of the firm had died.

La Clairière-Maredsous

Around 1971 we tested our ideas about sequential organisation and specialised spaces on a small cheap building which was urgently required and had to be both flexible and expandable. For this we adopted the SAR modular system developed by John Habraken at Eindhoven in a simplified version. A regular timber structure based on a 4.8 metre grid was set up, designed to span in either direction, but the perimeter was allowed to remain free and irregular. The flooring, with tiles already laid, provided regular bases for structural columns. Interchangeable facade elements of various sizes, specifications and colours were then set up independent of the columns, weaving in and out of them to create many angles and returns, often departing from the perimeter defined by the roof. It was a well organised job, and demountable elements were used only for small scale variations; even so these were numerous.

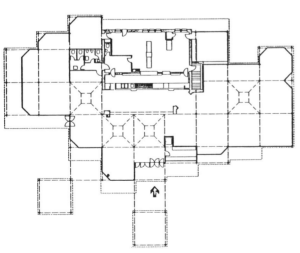

*Planning of Medical Faculty buildings,
Woluwé-St Lambert*
With the design and construction of Medical
Faculty buildings at Woluwé, Brussels, came our
first opportunity to explore the possibilities of
modular co-ordination properly as part of the
campaign for a more responsive industry. This is
the only building, to our knowledge, which has
been strictly designed on a grid of 10 cm with a

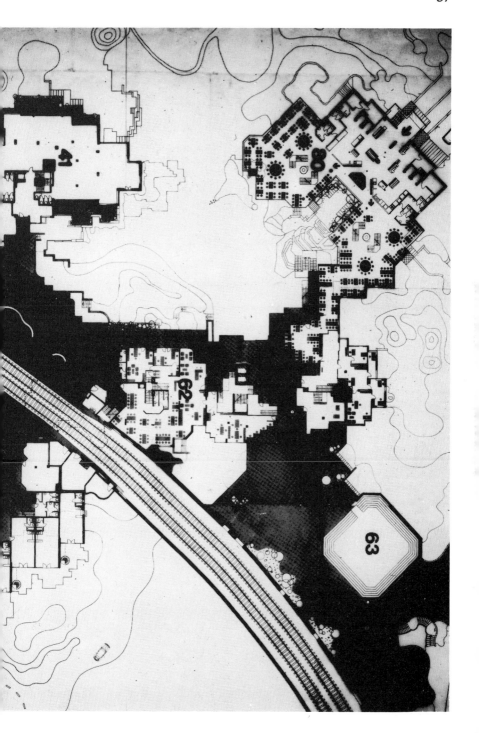

bias towards 30. The grid facilitated the organisation of a form of construction that was essentially traditional, while also allowing the inclusion of a great diversity of forms in a reasonably straightforward manner. It proved to be before its time: this was industrial architecture without industrialists.

The Social Centre (Mémé)

The history of the project is well known: in the late '60s the Catholic University decided to move its medical faculties from Louvain to Brussels, and consulted the students and their organisation 'La Maison Medicale' (Mémé) about the new development. The student body suggested a more fluid kind of organisation than that already proposed, with its rigid zones and functional buildings, but the University proved unsympathetic. Disappointed, the students turned to our office, inviting us to design the buildings of their 'social zone' with their involvement. Thus arose the opportunity to conceive a varied series of buildings amounting to some 40,000 square metres floorspace, with direct participation by clients and inhabitants.

Today, with several years' hindsight, we are still trying to understand why we arrived at a solution to the industrial question which was so very different from that of other architects working in the same circumstances. Our motives, our political choices, and our attitudes – none of which are objective criteria – certainly diverged: these gave rise in turn to different mentalities. On that basis the product was inevitably different. The evolution of technique is not predestined, it is much more at the mercy of men's wishes and states of mind than of any inherent fate.

Faced with a set of disparate parts, the average practitioner begins by ignoring them or by suppressing the most extreme, then he

It would not be appropriate in the present text to describe in detail our extraordinary collaboration with students, authorities and technical specialists, the process by which it was achieved, the conflicts and reconciliations. However, the reader may imagine the proliferation of wishes, the extraordinarily diverse ways of life which had to be incorporated in the buildings, resulting in a style of architecture which avoids repetition, severity, and the usual professional limitations.

The intelligent and friendly organisation of industry which we had conceived would make such quantity and diversity possible. To start with we would need a rigorous form of modular coordination, derived from SAR but modified through debate: we had already tested it several times in live projects.

reduces them to one or a series of types for which he can propose model solutions – the artificial average of the statistician. For him the rest remains marginal, exceptional, unimportant. In consequence he can dominate and he can industrialise. Our motives were precisely the opposite: we sought the greatest possible differentiation, the avoidance of repetition, and

the opportunity to preserve a sense of the *genius loci* (one might call this situationist, perhaps). We instinctively avoided every kind of authoritarian imposition threatening the landscape: bureaucracy, closed working methods, isolation, factory processes, ordering systems etc. This did not amount to a deliberate renunciation of art or architecture but rather to acceptance of a world of openness, cooperation, osmosis, empathy, mimesis and fluidity. The

40

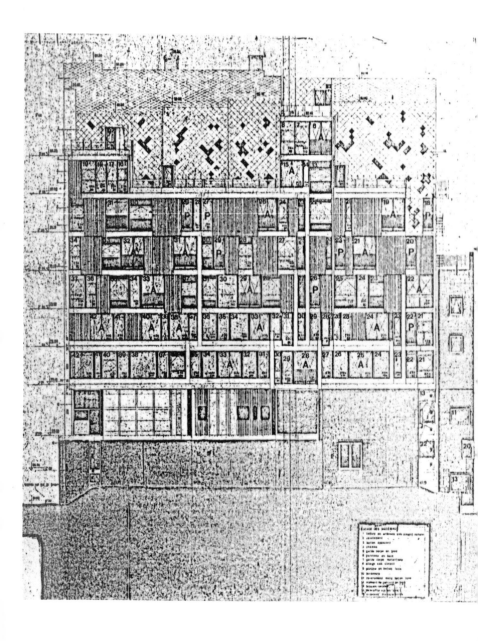

41

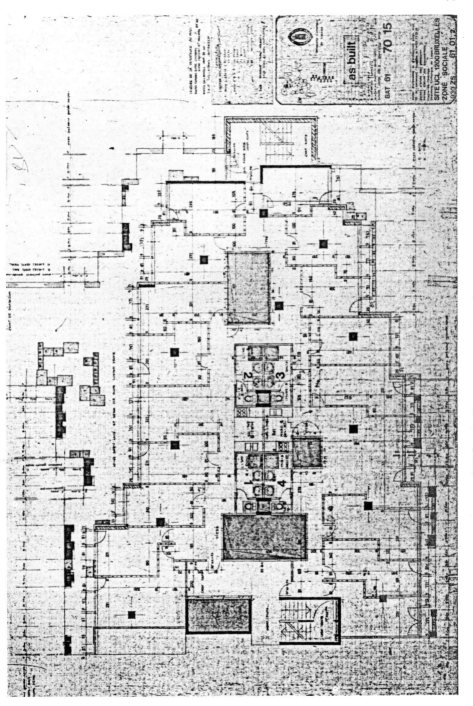

contractors and sub-contractors already offering industrial prefabrication proposed too heavy a technology to fit in with our approach. We needed to standardise at a different scale. This is how the question of components arose.

The wandering columns

As might be expected, we did not set up the columns on a regular grid, yet neither did we leave their placing to chance. They are set at multiples of 90 cm, forming a mosaic of square or rectangular umbrellas which support each other at the edges, each having its own personality in terms of size, form and position. The reasoning behind this arrangement is straightforward. Why line them up in rows when it is not necessary? The architecture influences the behaviour of the

The whole group of buildings is regulated by a single grid so fine in scale that its presence is well-nigh imperceptible.

inhabitants: regular columns make them con-
formist, irregular ones stimulate the imagination.
If all columns are spaced at 6 metres, then all the
rooms are likely to end up at 3 metres. If spacings
vary in both directions without repetition of the
regulating dimension (for even when concealed,
it makes itself felt), then the plan of each room
can be different. Must such an approach be
defeated by the technical difficulties it
generates? We have complicated the spaces,
spans, perimeters and floor openings. The
spaces develop in response to all kinds of
pressures rather than according to a single
principle: we have called this 'wandering
columns', and it is the most complex form which
can best welcome and reinforce a varied arrangement of spaces and connections. The kind of
communication which they induce is that of
chosen contacts rather than of endured
hierarchy: a network rather than a tree-structure,
a sponge rather than an abacus.

Maison Medicale (Mémé), typical floor plan

From the start of the project we had difficulties
over this with our structural engineers. In the
Mémé, our first test-building, we chose the
principle of slab floor (or mushroom floor): a floor
of uniform thickness (as our light partitions ran in
all directions) with the slab made extra thick
(permitting inclusion, incidentally, of wiring,
plumbing and heating) and the columns extra fat
to avoid punching through. With less labour and
more concrete this floor proved economical – the
stresses are considered as continuous and not
analysed one by one: it is a technique involving
considerable structural redundancy and it would
doubtless be difficult to calculate it for a
maximum structural efficiency and economy of
means. Seen as if by X-ray the layers of
reinforcement should present a precise and un-
broken pattern of known or expected stresses:
an image of the building's strength.

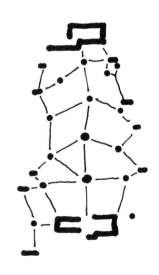

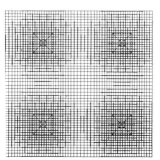

Robert Maillart: plan view of the reinforcement for mushroom columns.

Slab floors

This technique seemed to us obvious if a little naive: for our engineers it was irrational, expensive, and troublesome. They complained to the clients, 'This will cost 47.5% more', a measure of their anger rather than of the concrete. They were wrong, for calculations proved it to be economical. It was not simply a technical or economic argument, though, but was concerned more fundamentally with states of mind. Without prejudice, we knew only too well the kind of analytical logic to which they were wedded; however, they never came to understand or accept our kind of fluid, intuitive and global logic. In addition they put in a claim floor by floor for an expensive and inelegant computer program used to make rigorous calculations of our complexities.

Arbitration

A representative of the university who understood our problem found a suitable arbitrator and pourer of oil on troubled waters: our engineer's old computer programming professor. He spoke consolingly to his suffering colleague: 'First imagine the columns regularly spaced, calculate them to the average, then add reinforcement where you think it is needed: I'm confident that your engineering instinct will see you through . . .' Thus we obtained our 'wandering columns', and the engineer succeeded in concealing the 'ghost beams' as stressed bands within the thickness of the slab. His persistent instinct for hierarchy led him to reorganise the elements into specialist roles, carrying and carried, 'master' beams and servile slabs, instead of the continuous reinforcement acting step by step and from centre to centre devised by Robert Maillart who invented the mushroom column. He had deceived us but was surprised when we told him so. A good relationship was established, and after that our engineer proved most reliable.

The building shell was irregular and heterogeneous: concrete and masonry structures with lightweight additions and infill in timber, all on the 10 + 20 cm grid derived from SAR. With the addition of staircases to the masonry walls on the north and south sides and the lift shaft this simple structure already promised complex possibilities. At this stage, in principle, the building is finished: it is only necessary to add demountable window frames, moveable partitions and prefabricated sanitary units, to lay carpets and services (some already included in the shell), to add beds, chairs and tables, and finally the students. The structure endures but the infill is soon out of date: thus we make it removable.

Restaurant: change of direction,
the grid pivots

North side

Restaurant terrace

Administration and school, east side

Structure and infill

Two legal notions about property (or for that matter about use) are associated with these concepts, also two notions about authority and two deciding factors. One applies to the supporting structure, to the artificial ground which provides the raw space for development. In the same way as with real ground it consists both of supports – foundations, columns, bearing walls, floor slabs – and of various networks and connections: public lifts and stairs, hot and cold water, gas, electricity, heating, telecommunications, deliveries, rubbish collection, flues, air-conditioning etc. In all these matters the usual notions of co-ownership apply.

A floor in the Mémé before installation of partitions.

Students changing the partitions.

The other legal notion applies to the additions: these infill elements can be manufactured, put together by a craftsman or knocked up by the inhabitant himself. The structure should be conceived to allow these three possibilities to take place simultaneously or subsequently, and to encourage the inhabitants to take the initiative: thus dwelling plans should always differ, and so should finishes. Typically a claustrophobic inhabitant might like large windows while an agoraphobic one would buy small ones.

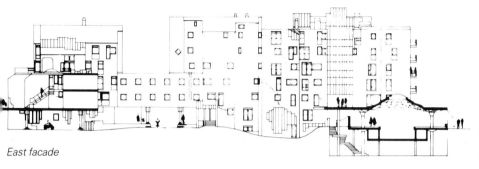

East facade

In this way one firm equipped for large scale construction could be employed to complete the empty shell providing the 'artificial sites', while separate smaller concerns undertook the service networks and finishes. These operations could be divided geographically into distinct blocks and in set time sequences: for example, several joiners for each section of framing, partitions and doors, and not one joiner each confined respectively to the exterior, the interior and the partitions. The specification divides into independent sections.

Even with diversity industrialised building can be unacceptable, unless softened with interventions by craftsmen or inhabitants and taken over by plants.

South side

Along the Avenue de l'Assomption

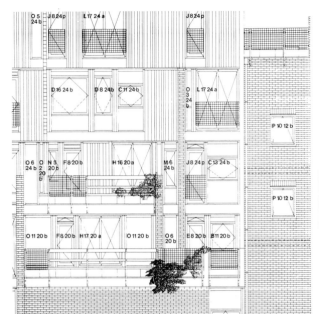

Facade with grid

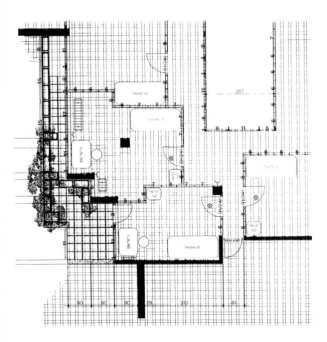

Plan with grid

Catalogue of windows used as self-adhesive sheets

Services

Technical services are not put in in the traditional way. The input and discharge of fluids take place at several locations: this can be approached in various ways. Nowhere yet have we found sanitary components which can be installed as a complete sub-assembly. Cables for lighting and communications run in the slab and emerge independent of the movable partitions in service areas or at points foreseen as advantageous, and

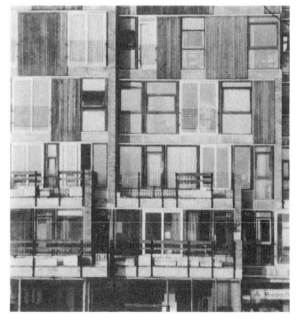

from such points they run within the living space or in provisional ducts. We proprosed treating the hot water radiator system the same way, with fixed delivery points and flexible hoses, but dropped the idea after the panic it caused among our engineers.

One of the 'attics'

Joinery

The external joinery was at first selected from catalogues, but we found that organised craftsmen could do it cheaper. We included all kinds of openings in sizes which were multiples of 30 cm (– 10 cm to allow for the ends of partitions). We allowed for all kinds of materials (wood, aluminium, plastics) and for cans of stain and paint of every shade. The elements were placed on the facades in a disordered way relating to an equally diverse and haphazard arrangement of rooms within. Lacking a roulette wheel or a computer programmed to produce random combinations we used playing cards: often however the architect is better at simulating chance than such tools, and he does not make mistakes.

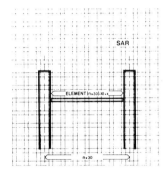

The SAR module

Here, in brief, is what we kept of the SAR module and of its advantages within the politics of international standards which already set the module for construction at 10 cm. Stichting Architectural Research was set up around 1965, financed by a group of large Dutch architects' offices and professional bodies. Its goal was to explore the possibilities of standardising primary structures, the essential supporting elements, both in building and planning terms. Such standardisation was intended to facilitate the use of industrial elements in the secondary construction, to encourage diversity in mass-produced dwellings, and open up the possibility of modifications and replacements with components of different life-spans. N.J. Habraken, the principal designer of the SAR system, saw that the contemporary mass-produced dwelling could only be made in a way which denied the inhabitant any say in its design. If one considers his participation indispensable, Habraken argued, one must re-think the whole operation, distinguishing at the start between public and private domains and controlling interaction between them. When the individual has no say, the result is oppressive, but equally if there is no public role, one ends up with chaos. This was a problem of organisation, of decision-making rather than of technique. The primary structure should be independent of the infill; the SAR module controls the dimensions of elements, defining the space into which they fit, and the relationship each has with its neighbour.

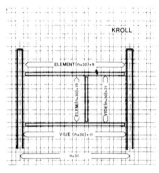

Our reinterpretations of the SAR module
The SAR rules concerning grids (10 + 20) for location of elements and allowance of tolerances seemed to us straightforward and necessary. We only kept the 'paired series' of structures (set on the axis of the 20 cm band), rejecting the improbable 'unpaired series' (on the 10 cm band). We suppressed the tolerance gap of the adjusting dimension through proposing that elements be standardised at multiples of 10 cm, dimensions generous enough in scale for each element to allow its neighbour to fit in easily, just as a wardrobe 99 cm wide can fit into a niche of 101 cm.

We never succeeded in getting our engineers to adopt this fine scale of modular coordination: they could see no reason to favour any particular dimension, and they could not understand the necessity of the centimetre gap between contained and container. They only understood 'nominal' dimensions.

We also abandoned SAR's specialised 'functional zones'. This we did without regret, for such a system only meant that industrial components tended to be made to different dimensions according to whether they were intended for one zone or another: the elements also tended to be too large. We dropped the rules

East side.

provisionally, expecting that programmes of a more mechanical nature such as offices, factories and laboratories would demand their reinstatement, yet as people occupy these kinds of building too, a fine scale of dimensions would again be appropriate.

In housing a 30 cm module is barbaric, and even 10 cm is too large: 2.5 cm or 1 cm would be more ideal. What we ended up with was an

Rotation of the grid

arrangement whereby supporting elements usually 20 cm thick were set at multiples of 30 cm to create spaces which were multiples of 10 cm (n.30 + 10, −10, or n.30 precisely, without hierarchy or moral implication). The floor levels were also standardised at 2.7 or 3.6 m, so that service pipes, external panels and staircases could be prefabricated to the same height as sanitary and technical units (which nobody wants to prefabricate any more for fear of being constrained by an intolerable degree of repetition).

ACC/SAR: virtues and vices of two modular systems

In France the ACC, 'L'Association Construction et Composants', proposed a standard whereby interior spaces are set on a grid of 30 cm from wallpaper to wallpaper. It seems to have been devised for the benefit of decorators, for either it necessitates disruption of the grid or it involves four different dimensions – the maximum and minimum wall thickness, or twice the maximum thickness. The SAR module, by contrast, makes the axes of the bearing elements dominant: it might have been devised by the masons or bricklayers!

When the bearing walls contain the space according to the ACC grid, the addition of an extra partition wall breaks the system. While the SAR is conceived for blocks with multiple bays and lightweight facades, the ACC module has to be thought of more in terms of a row of boxes.

One might be tempted to believe that the ACC sets up a grid perfectly adapted to accept standardized fittings – partitions, kitchen furniture, sanitary units, stairs etc. – but this is an illusion. Partitions can easily be fitted to the nearest centimetre, and kitchen furniture can be adjusted with adaptor elements: after 1955 there were no further studies on 'wet cells' fixing all sanitary functions in one unit, while staircases depend more on storey heights and never fit in conveniently with a 30 cm module. Thus there is no need for the dimensions of fittings to dictate the geometry of the enclosing structure.

In addition, the ACC has never properly taken

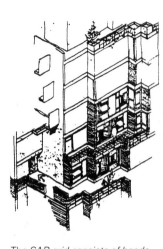

The SAR grid consists of bands 10 and 20 cm wide running in both directions, the module being 10 cm with a 30 cm bias. The 10 cm band always becomes an adjustment space between primary structure and secondary elements, since both begin and end within it. The distance to be negotiated, that is the space remaining between grid and element, (not to be confused with tolerance space) always ends up as less than 10 cm. This negotiable band is useless with 'hard' components which are standardised and require precise placing, but in reality it tends to be generalised. It prohibits some overall dimensions (45, 105 cm). It groups dimensions in two series, as a result of the fact that primary structure follows the centre line of the 10 or 20 cm band. In section, it runs in 20 cm steps beginning with the floor surface.

into account the rules of joints and tolerances necessary if components are to be installed without running into difficulty over details. Also, the task of adjusting the size of dwellings in 30 cm steps, which can amount to + or − some 2.00 m^2 per dwelling, can prove impossible when controls on surface area are tight.

A classroom

The playground

Adjustable partitions in a school: postscript

A primary school had become embedded in the two floors of the building containing dwellings and local administration. At that time we were just recovering from another painful experience in the educational realm, when we had proposed discussing the question of movable partitions with the pupils, and the Head, quite horrified, had thrown us out. However, at Woluwé we were on good terms with the teachers, who allowed us to visit their classrooms and discuss things with pupils. Cautiously we set up movable partitions throughout. We used the same partitions as those between student rooms: identical in composition, dimensions, acoustic performance and fitting. The client was sceptical of their practical benefit, but accepted them since they were within the agreed cost limits. He seemed to be justified in his doubts, for the partitions were never moved: all that happened was that a couple of offices were converted into a classroom.

Ten years later the teachers and representatives of the University, which was both client and owner, returned to us. They had a problem: they needed two extra classrooms but had no funds for an extension. There was only one way out: remove the partitions and reorganise the space to fit in with new requirements. Thus in the end the movable partition system did serve a purpose.

This mobility was pursued initially for two reasons: most obviously and primarily to allow evolutionary change, but above all also to allow users to create their own spaces as they had already done 10 years earlier thanks to an 'industrial' product. As might be expected not a single teacher remained from that previous era, but contact had not altogether been lost. Given a fresh opportunity, we opted to make no decisions ourselves, to propose nothing too precise, but rather to present possibilities and supply encouragement. A synthesis should arise at the end of our consultation.

Model at scale 1:20

We constructed a model large and robust enough to be manipulated by a dozen children at a time. Our first aim was that they should recognise it as their school, and they did so immediately. They added at the correct scale tables, chairs, sink, cupboards, cushions, lamps on the ceiling and finally their teacher and themselves. After that they started moving partitions to make some classrooms larger, improve others, add two more, and reduced the Head's office to the size of a box-room, all in a unified operation. Each class took up and improved on the work of the previous class, sticking the partitions into the cork floor, and coming to grips with the rules of the modular grid much more readily than our engineers.

The final decisive session involved the teachers, who proved quite open to the children's suggestions and prepared to accept a variegated solution. With people who are committed and interested, participation is straightforward and enjoyable.

They watch themselves on video

Le Bernalmont

Around 1978 some of the Liège authorities (for social housing, industrial promotion, Walloon regional development, etc.) set up a study group for the redevelopment of an abandoned coal-mining area near Liège known as 'Le Bernalmont'. The group set up a competition for 250 of the 2500 dwellings planned and demanded that they be constructed of components available from Walloon industries. We decided to take part in this competition to put to the test within particular local conditions what we had learned through our projects and experiments. We had no hope of winning, for we were already all too familiar with the oppressive ways of public local authorities and their dull mediocrity. Besides, the jury included members with an obstinate leaning towards an eighteenth century image which they believed to be rationalist.

Some young and energetic engineer-architects catalogued all the local components available. They proposed to put together an illustrated booklet, also including a dimensional coordinating system, performance specifications and cost analysis. This promised to be quite a remarkable legal and technical document. They hoped that industrial thinking and organisation would reduce costs, and we hoped at the same time that it would result in an appropriately complex architecture.

The local style

Industrial components are unknown in Belgium. Heavy prefabrication lurks beyond its frontiers, but general colonisation has been avoided thanks largely to passive resistance by the populace, who have remained resolutely unsympathetic. Large-scale construction has also been limited by an improvement grant system, set up in preference to social housing bodies which too often grow excessively large and unresponsive.

The existing landscape

The competition amply demonstrated the misunderstandings and inflexibility of jury members. These included politicians who knew little of architecture, prefabricated construction or components, but held nevertheless a conventional enough view of the authoritarian image which a public institution should transmit when building for charitable purposes. There were also engineers on the jury, and though they were familiar with the world of components, they showed no clear understanding of the architectural freedom which such a system could allow. One might have expected more from the architect jury members, but they showed a poor knowledge of components, had difficulty in distinguishing them from the world of heavy prefabrication, and tamely believed the production of an oppressively repetitive image to be inevitable.

Our aims

Despite the strange circumstances of such a competition, it provided us with an ample opportunity to apply our ideas and test research we had done elsewhere. The participation of possible future inhabitants would introduce an element of local contemporary culture and a welcome variety which could easily be constructed with a component system because of the industrial base. Thus we could adopt a wide range of dimensions, types of material and structure, allow for spontaneous extensions, organise strict construction sequences, remain within the budget, and include the work of traditional craftsmen.

After we had met the officials from the study group and their families who were to act as inhabitants for the purposes of the competition, we went to see the local action committee which was openly opposed to the municipality. We wanted to check on our interpretation of what we had already seen and gain a fresh point of view: the social housing office, for example, had refused to give us the names of families on their housing list. Why?

'We don't want a concrete jungle and high densities; we would rather people were allowed to live as they wish. We don't want demolition, road-widening, tall blocks, ghettos, social housing: instead we would like gardens, allotments, variety – no rigidity. Old houses should be kept, priority be given to pedestrians, and the new architecture should be sympathetic to the needs of women and children, of old people, the handicapped, and those with large families. We need green space, trees, benches, recreation areas, places for ball games and social and cultural facilities. Traffic should be made to go slowly and public transport be readily available. Dwellings should be affordable, and small workshops and businesses should be allowed to coexist with the housing. We would like cafés and places to play petanque. We need to get away from the image of mass-developments with their communal entrances, their relentless stacking of dwellings, their colourless and grime-stained walls.' All this emerged by degrees at a series of meetings.

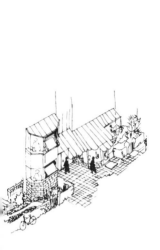

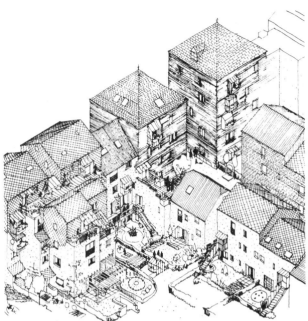

Our response

Our first reaction was to mix up all the different types of dwelling: this would help us avoid the programmed homogeneity characteristic of new towns. We would also vary the density, for if some buildings are made very compact, others can be left almost detached. The latter are the most popular with buyers whose capital can help set the whole operation in motion, and the variety that results from such pockets of low density helps produce an impression of freedom, ease and transition, making a walk through this organic type of development a more rewarding experience.

Instead of following the usual model for a block of flats with its stacks of identical dwellings, we proposed clusters of maisonettes, as often as possible with single entrances. Above we placed one storey of flats, and on top of that a further cluster of maisonettes with the upper storey in the roof. This arrangement avoids the need for lifts since the highest entry is only on the third floor. Clean well-lit cellars provide extension possibilities for the ground floor and for communal use.

Division into maisonettes facilitates the inclusion at a private scale of services often provided communally, such as cellars or places for rubbish bins, bicycles and prams. The largest families can be housed on the ground floor, and so can any non-residential functions.

Furthermore, this type of organisation leaves spaces which can be taken over, thus preventing

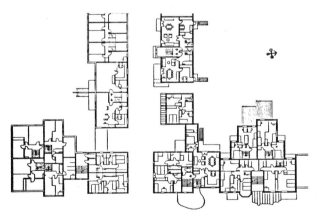

Ground floor plan

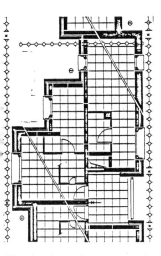

Plan showing various structural elements

the inhabitants from feeling cornered. They can make the additions themselves or call in local craftsmen, altering the spaces intended for such possibilities, such as the cellars and attics, without getting involved in difficult external works: it is like the air space left within an egg. On the outside the architecture is intended to accept extensions at both front and rear and not to inhibit them through its initial form: the building will pursue its own course of evolution. Our illustration shows how it might be after 25 years: we keep this image very much in mind to prevent ourselves creating an architecture which is too finite.

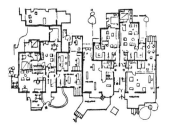

25 years later

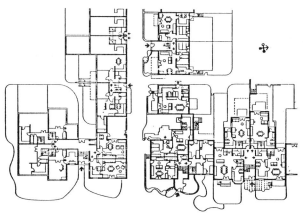

First floor plan

The price of diversity

We were firm in our conviction that diversity is not necessarily expensive, but how could one prove it? It seems to us so essential to the nature of an open industry, that an architecture failing to exploit such diversity can only be a shameful perpetuation of the old heavy prefabrication: repetition has become anachronistic.

For the majority of constructional elements this is self-evident – for colours, cladding, window frames, doors, positioning of light partitions, etc. It is less so with the larger structural elements. We discussed this with the technical staff of several firms in Liège who had already considered the problem: they knew as we did that the cost of panels is determined above all by the perfection required of their moulds. This perfection makes every turn, angle or junction in the mould very expensive. When the requirements are less exacting, for instance in a structural element which will later be covered up, some roughness and approximation can be tolerated. It is then quite easy to develop a mould with quickly variable sides which can be fixed at 30 cm intervals without further adjustment, as in our Project IB. The mock-ups of doors and windows used to create openings are also much easier to vary when the datum lines can remain exposed after moulding. There are no special cavities or services included in the panel.

These less sophisticated techniques allow for a more economical operation. One can make several such installations or even prefabricate elements on site under a temporary shelter within direct range of a crane. Then the factory is on site.

Modular coordination
The Bernalmont project was first organised according to the SAR grid (10 and 30 cm), then according to the ACC system, somewhat cruder at 30 cm (and 10 cm vertically), adding necessary tolerances. Envelope elements fitted on tangentially and could not be geared to a module without averaging out the numerous disruptions of the grid which upset them.

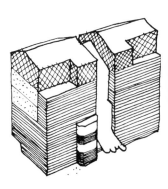

Varied materials

Heterogeneous structures
*Next we renounced the fixed
systematic skeleton to be filled in,
which often turned out more
expensive (and less flexible) than
prefabricated walls. Then we
superimposed three construction
systems according to their
particular virtues. Either heavy
panels prefabricated in concrete
and insulated on the exterior, or
concrete walls, carried in turn
lighter walls in cellular concrete,
while top floors were build in
timber frame, surmounted by a
timber roof structure.*

Semi-industrial firms

We visited firms in the region to discuss our technical proposals, to see whether they were appropriately equipped, and we soon confirmed our suspicions that a panel capable of carrying external and internal finish with insulation built-in and watertight joints was bound to be both expensive and risky. It would be much easier to make external walls with the same sized elements but poured joints, not attempting to make them watertight but filling the holes and covering the surface with render. The panels could be formed with voids and recessions, but without projections, for it is essential to reduce work on the mould to the minimum. Under such conditions the small local prefabricator could compete in the market, and avoid all the problems of tooling up at a vast scale and distributing the over-abundant product to a disproportionately large area.

Our proposition

Allowing for variation in programme, form, material, technique, outline, context and potential additions, our method remains essentially open, reserving a variety of techniques for choice on site. We also wanted to include other long-standing concerns of ours: the work of craftsmen and their inimitable self-expression, the parallel presence of plant life which should be nurtured by the residents, and the addition of decorative elements in appropriate places by popular choice.

We were reasonably sure that a complexity which was easy to add to would kindle the creativity of those who lived there as they became familiar with their surroundings, and we hoped that the development would take on a life of its own, autonomous and self-regulating. In reality it came to nothing. As had been implied all along, the winner could only be 'uniform'.

We knew only too well that our 'populist' intentions would antagonise those in charge, while our consultation of the inhabitants would scarcely endear us to them. In addition, the populist image only helped to mask the practical and rational side of our work which had already been so well worked out with the help of local firms. Should one therefore resort to disguises? And then in any case . . .

Floors

Heavy floors were to be constructed with slabs cast in situ, or with precast units mounted dry in various sizes based on multiples of 30 cm both ways: floors in maisonettes might also be in wood or steel. The choice of material for walls and floors was to be left as late as possible without having to change the drawings, whose reference dimensions remained nominal. Each material received an appropriate cladding, so the diversity of structure would be expressed visually in the landscape.

We were doubtful of finding prefabrication firms large enough (and without a monopoly) to take on big spans (6.00 m) as cheaply as average ones. For centuries domestic rooms have had a width of 3.00 to 4.50 m: we preferred to follow this precedent and decided that floors should normally be carried on all four walls to reduce reinforcement, sometimes even adding a central column. Such conditions proved more economical, more open to small prefabrication firms and more immediately realisable than the absent-minded practice of architects who restrict themselves to one direction of span, often the least advantageous one. Dreaming of an abstract industry, they penalise their projects with unnecessary expenditure on structure built-in at such an early stage that modification is not practicable. Their obsession betrays a reductive attitude: two sides are used for bearing, the other two for daylight. This is absurd, for one must be able to make holes in the bearing sides and to fill in the open ones. In addition this system results in unacceptable and costly repetition. To run the structure in all directions is richer and more complex: it implies an architecture of interlocking elements, of continuity, which adapts itself more readily to local conditions.

Nieuwegein

In 1979 Bouwfonds (a housing association) and the municipality of Nieuwegein near Utrecht asked us to prepare a project for around 60 dwellings sited close to the future centre, involving participation with future inhabitants. The site lay between a major road, a small canal planned to enliven the area, and two existing

Roofs
We proposed several types of roof, but always inhabited and made accessible, with ceilings partly following the slope under raised ties or using preconstructed roof sections to eliminate site carpentry. The roofs were to be finished in all types of local materials, and pitches differed from place to place, producing a varied landscape. Wherever possible, upper floors would open onto terraces. There were few projecting balconies: they complicate construction and the construction sequence as well as generating insulation problems. We prefer that they should be added afterwards, perhaps even 10 years later.

buildings on the corners which we could build up against, a welcome presence which reduces the inevitable isolation of such new-town blocks.

The programme included tall narrow town houses on the old Amsterdam model, if possible with gardens, and flats with balconies or terraces. The ground floor rooms at the centre of the plot would be given over to shops, workshops, and meeting places. We approached the Dutch regulations about habitability and floor areas with interest: these are very standardised but mainly sensible and more generous in scope than those of a few years back.

The association added a room of 9 m^2 to each dwelling, which was to be made flexible according to a simple rule: the residents should decide among themselves whether they wanted to turn it into a private office or study, or whether they should connect it to the next room belonging to a neighbour, or even to two or three others, to create a communal space. These interchangeable rooms were to connect always with the most public parts of each dwelling: living room, hall or attic. Extensions were also to be possible both front and rear using traditional masonry construction.

A coordination system similar to SAR is adopted automatically. The constructional system devised in observance of the draconian budget for social housing in Holland is based on a standard framework set to a daily rhythm of two spans, which needless to say are identical. They told us, 'In Holland, the dimension is 5.40 m'. Typically, the in-situ walls are later cased in brick and the tips of the gables are linked by beams which produce regular pitched roofs. It is this system which produces long rows of individual houses in Holland which all look the same.

Since two frames are made at a time, we asked, could one not base them on different dimensions and apply them haphazardly to break the repetition? The technicians had no ready answer: nobody had ever asked them this before. To our surprise, it proved possible to adopt two dimensions, 4.50 m and 5.40 m, within the same costs, and to mix them.

To create more diversity we set up a list of 24 variables which, subject to the residents' choice, could create an image less obviously 'new town'. We worked out variations of volume with the Dutch technicians before finally putting together blocks of flats and smaller houses.

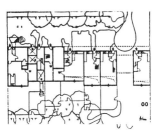

Whether it is industrial or traditional, a system of construction which is too restricted represses any desire to give character to the development: one must superimpose on it another system organised differently, which remains compatible with it but provokes a network of small scale

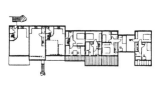

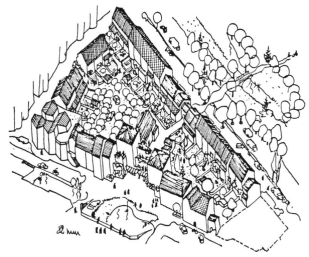

incidents. At the scale of the neighbourhood this is the same kind of complexity as that produced at the Mémé by our 'wandering columns'.

After all our efforts, the housing market in Holland then slumped, and the association shelved the project.

An entrance made by craftsmen

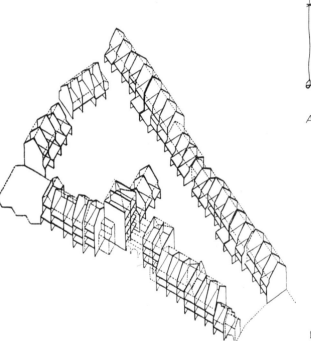

Perspective showing walls

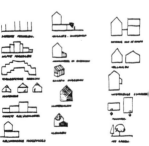

Differences

4 A SEMI-INDUSTRIAL APPROACH

One instance: 'The Oaks' at Emerainville

In 1979 the new town of Marne La Vallée invited us to devise a project involving experiment in two interacting fields: user participation and system building. The programme comprised 80 flats with balconies and 30 individual houses, all based on system construction. The 30 houses were to be designed wherever possible in consultation with their buyers. We were to examine the possibility of using industrial components both for primary structure and for secondary elements, and to adopt them in preference to traditional methods if the price proved competitive.

The site

1. 'Architecture cloaque' and 'urbanisme cloaque' are here rendered as 'sewer architecture' and 'sewer planning'. 'Cloaca' in Latin can mean a sewer or the anal passage of an animal. I suggested the alternative translation 'intestinal architecture' for its image of endless pipes carrying fluids, pipes that are normally concealed. This carries the sense of obsession with servicing and a kind of digestion which Kroll intends, but he considered it insufficiently pejorative. (PBJ)

Our sly engineering

How is mass housing usually conceived? First the dwelling types are worked out in detail, then they are lined up and piled up around stairs and service stacks. There is no reason to avoid serial repetition, left-right handing and simple accumulation, since all elements are identical. Thus, ever obedient to the dictates of its digestive systems, arises a 'sewer architecture'.

The same kind of thinking applies also at a large scale: the blocks are set up according to rules governing roads, sewers and other services, always with a tree-like hierarchical organisation rather than a network. Even when architects try to alleviate the situation with more lively geometries they cannot avoid producing 'sewer planning'.[1]

To avoid the 'sewer' approach, one can start by interspersing single houses amongst the blocks of flats. If these are based on town-house types they can facilitate the transition between the two. This achieved, we then design the flats, but we vary them according to size, position, and connections in ways that appeal to us. We do produce handed versions, but with a differing orientation we vary both layout and fenestration. We avoid dominant central staircases, preferring to set the dwellings side by side or one above the other in less rigid ways, sometimes creating maisonettes, sometimes clusters, always through empathy and not by sheer calculation. The approaches to the dwellings remain dispersed and independent: no mechanical ordering, and little centralised management.

It is not our policy to give priority to roads and services – these can be arranged after the clusters are determined. This was only achieved through considerable effort, for our services engineers threw their hands up in horror and declared it impossible. We had therefore to study the servicing ourselves, making corrections here and there, but altering our plans only where arrangements had proved impossible. This was done without a general strategy, dealing with each case in particular: thus can the organic prevail. Distances and views for each space can be negotiated, adjusted until the necessary relationships are achieved: there is no geometrical regimentation, only a small scale organisation set up step by step. The same applies to the variegated external cladding, determined by personal preference and local circumstances, each individual move provoking the next in a contagious display of self-expression.

There are two areas of special significance in a dwelling: the main entrance and the exit to garden or terrace. The former will not simply be a hole punched in an abstract wall, but will be decorated: with faience, a brick surround, a patterned render, the whitest concrete, boulders – more than just décor, almost a liturgy. The

The early inhabitants
One can well imagine an operation in which a group of concerned people would define the major moves in reorganising the landscape collectively, after which each one in turn would determine the layout and character of his dwelling. One by one these pioneers might then disappear, being replaced gradually by new inhabitants who would carry on the shared tradition. It is not in any way necessary that such a development should come to fruition in the presence of all its founding inhabitants. The signs of their personal expression in the built form provide a precious continuity, a promise of habitability which encourages newcomers to contribute in their turn. It is the way people care about their living space and express that care that preserves the living continuity of an urban texture, and which prevents it becoming an alien object placed among others of its kind according to an artificial geometry.

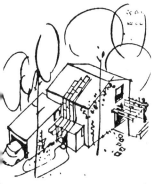

doorway from the living-room to the garden or terrace will convey more of an impression of verdure, perhaps with more emphasis on greenish tints, and a pergola to support real plants. Terraces will be loaded like library shelves, with a variety of possessions, potted plants, bicycles, screens etc.

Road networks in a soft landscape
To avoid generating the image of a landscape dominated by road networks two measures are essential. First one must get rid of the road as object with its aggressive hardware; it must become instead a space commanded by facades or other presences. Second, the architect should decide all the technical issues (and know them well) without having to exhaust himself trying to impose his vision of the landscape on specialists wedded to their technical armoury. He should also be able to let plants encroach upon his built world without ordering them too geometrically.

Networks within networks
If the various road networks serve layouts which they have not dominated through their own organisation, they will take the form of true networks and not tree-like structures which are always inherently hierarchical.

In search of an industrialised process
We looked through the literature of approved construction systems and soon found one which seemed hypothetically workable, our impression being confirmed on further investigation. The company representatives proved open-minded, friendly and curious; despite the constraints of their system it did not preclude acceptable architecture. Above all they had plenty of experience, their prices were competitive, and they could undertake the whole job. Perhaps this had something to do with the fact that two of their three prefabricated concrete plants were then standing idle. But in any case they had the added advantage that their factory was close to our site. We adopted them and went on to work together over several years. The system is complicated to manipulate, with its enormous beams and exposed joints between panels. At first sight its operation seems precise, rigid, and prohibitive of variety, but by degrees in the course of our discussions fresh possibilities emerged which could not have been foreseen at the start, and it proved possible to achieve almost the degree of variety that we sought.

We also investigated the possibilities of ten or so other systems, for two reasons. First, we wished to test the freedom they would allow and the modifications they would impose on our project; second, we wanted to compare performances in both technical and commercial terms.

We redesigned one pilot building for each system in turn and sent it to the firm concerned for their opinion. When we had received their reaction we visited each to check up on our work. To their dismay we had to tell them in the end that the operation would be reliably workable only with the first system.

Competition

When he can act independently of the producer, the role of the designer can affect the economic balance. It seems to be generally accepted that systems can escape the test of public tendering, as all too often they just turn out to be a means of handling the market opportunistically and avoiding competition. However, if architects are not tied to one system in particular, they can latch on to others without too much trouble. The current procedure for developing architecture through systems is approximately as follows. The client reaches an oral agreement with an industrialist to use his system on a project, provided that the price is right. The industrialist then looks into it, and only after he has made his study is the architect brought in, being expected to use the system within constraints already determined. He is almost obliged to turn out a design which is but a light variant of that already prefigured by the industrialist. And should he try to force the system beyond the convenience of the industrialist, he is accused of breaking the cost limit and finds he is fighting a losing battle: he simply has too little room for manoeuvre.

It seems as if construction systems must determine both architecture and the inhabitants' way of life according to the social, political and aesthetic model from which they derive, and which in turn they reproduce. The tendering

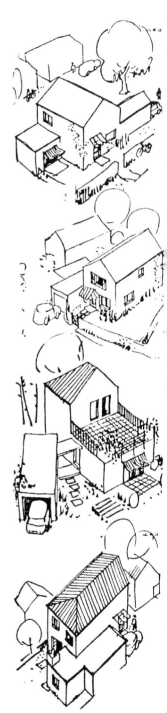

Compatibility

Having no responsibility for promoting the construction industry, we tend to push the systems we use to their extreme limits without respect for the way they could be used most easily, as we wish to achieve the greatest diversity of plan for a given simplicity of construction. To be sure of the component character of the chosen system we have superimposed another kind of construction on top of it which is very much a component system: timber framing. This also has the advantage of allowing a fourth storey on a concrete system limited to three and introduces the possibility of complete maisonettes in timber.

process should offer the architect a wider choice, but it does not allow him enough time to choose between different construction systems. To devise and then to modify plans demands too much effort, for once techniques and materials are fixed, nothing can be changed. To adapt to a more or less industrial procedure, it is necessary first to describe it precisely and then to design following its rules. There tends to be no competition because nobody has the persistence or the time to review all the possibilities. Furthermore, if one construction system should prove inadequate, it takes time to take on another. We told our industrialist that with our computer it was easy to change from one system to another. This was only half true, but when he realised that we had already consulted ten others he took fright and lowered his prices. Competition played its part through these implied threats.

Realistic systems

Official support for construction systems goes no further than improvement of existing practice. The current preoccupation is to test established systems which are doubtless less experimental than some, but backed by considerable technical experience. Stuck firm in the current tradition of banal prefabrication, they try to improve it in its own terms, without drastic reconsideration.

It has to be acknowledged that the system we chose is a bit rigid and that its constraints are sometimes mean. For example, the choice of joinery is very limited, the placing of formers for such elements in the moulds prohibiting any variation of size or position. The standard dimensions used by the firm were determined quite accidentally by the conditions of their first job (even so, this probably leads to more lively results than does dry theory). The panel joints are very visible on the outside, and that is no advantage. The details of junctions between materials are sometimes clumsy, and we could not argue over all of them. The textures of concrete external panels are oppressive, but there is little choice. As soon as the plan departs from the rectangle, the system demands enormous beams 36 cm wide. The rotation involved in placing panels, which is associated with the fact that the bays are aligned always 15 cm off the grid, prohibits symmetry, but fortunately we were trying to avoid it anyway. Split levels and mezzanines greatly complicate panel organisation and demand feats of design. The fit between container and contained greatly affects costs: instinctively one turns to the cube or to standard spans of 6.00 m. Too hasty a conformity with the rules of construction debases any architecture produced by this system. Fortunately, though, the wooden elements, which are inherently more flexible, can follow the grid if necessary or depart from it, fitting in with the technical dimensions of

Timber frame and banality
We wanted to show the vulgarisation of timber frame, its capacity to produce an architecture which is both sensible and popular. It also lends itself to 'populism', to the possibility that the inhabitant might take over full responsibility for construction (quite the opposite of what has happened for the last few generations). Averaging out these simplicities, there is no reason (apart from intellectual indolence or conservatism) to repeat identical types: for the same expenditure of effort they could all be different. We can exploit it playfully to produce a rich landscape . . .

concrete elements without difficulty. The wooden cladding also allows a variety of external form which could not be achieved in concrete alone.

We tackled these constraints at some cost in effort, involving research, exploration, cost agreements, even, when necessary, starting again from scratch. In the end we were far from convinced that such a system could allow enough freedom to create a diverse architecture without too much of a struggle.

Prototypes for an industrial process

In the organisation both of our own studies and of the preparation and assembly of panels, we employed the prototype method with its movement forward and back, from beginning to end of the process. To start with we launched a study which was brought quickly and clumsily to its conclusion; this dummy run provided us with information for the future process concerning the point at which each partner is engaged: we could then set up a rough schedule. A purely theoretical organisation, by contrast, can only work efficiently in a repetitive operation, and not in a creative one.

In the same way on site all new construction elements should be tested as prototypes and remodelled for perfection and a good fit. Failing this the whole series of elements may be strung together according to an approximate placing: this kind of industrial attitude is often ignored by the usual construction professionals or rejected outright. They want to go ahead with large scale production immediately and assemble without interruption as with traditional construction, where the whole procedure is already well understood.

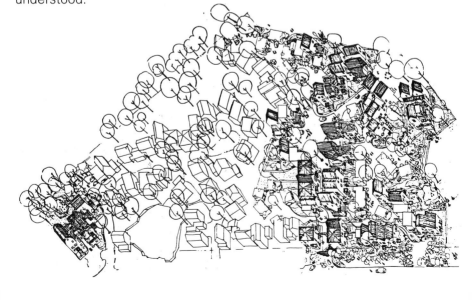

5 INDUSTRIAL COMPONENTS

Before they become a means of construction, components involve a redistribution of power and of roles, reversing the significance of what is built. If we fail to realise this we shall remain at the mercy of manufacturers of prefabricated systems who, knowing their products to be outdated, yet reintroduce them – renamed overnight – as components, taking advantage of the confusion.

The changeover from construction systems to components in the realm of building will be analogous to that in the engineering field, when it was first possible to construct things with interchangeable parts. The birth of the industrial component was marked by the first Remington guns, for any part would fit any gun. Construction still has not reached this point. Such interchangeability involves rules, co-ordination of dimensions and assembly sequences, detailed tolerances, production controls, so that products of remote factories operating autonomously can lend themselves easily to combination. It also requires a detailed economy of movements, materials and quality controls, and finally a market which is well understood, tested and organised.

Unfortunately almost all of those who still dream today of industrialised building merely perpetuate the sterile visions of Taylor and thus grind to a halt each time. We need to construct a habitat through industrial means, but architects instead use the habitat to pursue an industrial image. For it is not generally admitted that it will be useful to industrialise construction: but how can we know if we have not tried it? If the goal is seen as 'Construct cheap boxes which keep the rain out (or almost so) and which need express nothing beyond the means of their own production' – then heavy prefabrication can be counted successful enough. However, when a notion of cultural necessity is introduced, quite different criteria must apply. Walt Disney understood this aim in his own way much better than have generations of engineers. What was going on in the heads of all those enthusiasts for industrialisation in the 50s or even the 30s? 'The house is like a motor-car'. We have the standard model and the special, so some added 'there will be two kinds of architecture, the general and the specific'. The general is for schools, hospitals, offices, housing (the social realm): here let us reduce the number of models to a few types, and mass production will surely come into its own. Specific architecture on the other hand will include buildings of prestige, as a kind of alibi: thus architects preserved for themselves some of their old territory. And so the architecture of 1950 is perpetuated with a little cosmetic treatment. It is obviously a project designed to appeal to the industrialist. It promises an answer – though an inadequate one – to the question 'How should we industrialise?' when the essential question should be 'Why should we industrialise?'

And why precisely?

A few centuries ago builders saw no point in precise alignments, equal bay spacings, planar surface treatments or repetition of identical units. How have we moved from their creative liberty to our depressing repetitiveness and endless reiteration of those departures from human scale invented in the nineteenth century? We need have little doubt that it is neither industry nor the metric system which are to blame, but rather a kind of endemic blindness, a militaristic inability to distinguish between the necessary and the pernicious; this goes hand in hand with the destruction of cultural specificities through colonial conquest, and with the 'exploitation' of natural and human resources. It was the spirit of the age. However nothing (except perhaps bureaucracy) necessitates this degree of precision. It was necessary to wait until the period just after the First World War to see the emergence of forms which were supposedly industrial, accompanied by a theory which was also supposedly industrial. Yet on reflection, these forms and their supporting theories were only hymns to the gods of Industry, which in any case were not taken up in building until after the Second World War. Hymns reflecting a romanticism of rational appearance, following endless debate on the possibilities of industrialised artefacts, their uses at home and abroad, and on the need for modernity.

When industrialists eventually decided to interest themselves in building, it took the form of a watered-down regionalism: mass-produced bungalows. Industry can only produce in response to a social demand. Around 1950 it was necessary to build hurriedly, badly, and at a large scale: the programme was fulfilled. But at least at that time they were honest enough to propose demolition twenty years later. This was a 'proto-industrialisation' of building, mildly mechanised and sheltered from the rain, the workers designated as unskilled. It produced crude elements hastily piled up on mediocre sites stranded between roads and services.

Twenty years later the results have been acknowledged as demoralising. We no longer dare to put up 50 identical dwellings: instead we pepper the landscape with a series of house types equally lacking in any real connection with the place. The types make life easier for designers and administrators, but do nothing to improve industry or the landscape. One stage further on we find the construction system in which the old tools of heavy prefabrication have

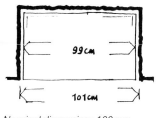

Nominal dimension: 100 cm

been modified a little to permit a degree of diversity, but the production runs are never adequate and the fiercest constraints always apply.

Cultural priority

Today the next stage is beginning, less industrial than cultural. An architectural imperative has arisen both at the scale of the landscape and of the building. In the end social pressure mobilises industry rather more effectively than industry's interest in its own survival.

This is precisely where many prophets of the construction industry are most mistaken, for they are too ready to sacrifice architecture in order to preserve industry. Most rely on abstractions which have been well purified of all bad habits (and of good ones at the same time), constructing new theoretical models (not dissimilar to the old ones) which aggessively reduce the numbers of elements and types (instead of taking advantage of the potential of mass production to increase them), thus leaving architects ever more hidebound. At the same time they rationalise mechanically according to preferential series dictated by mathematical reason, a system quite at odds with dimensions directly related to the body, for instance: 20 cm, 45, 72, 205, 250, 360 (plate, chair, table, door, ceiling height, width of a living room).

Taking the opposite approach, it would be necessary to draw out a scale including all dimensions necessary for any architecture: to start with perhaps, the unlimited 10 cm grid allowing all thicknesses. One would soon find that certain dimensions were used more frequently than others, and these would provide a more intelligent basis for setting up a module than the mathematical abstractions proposed by most organisers of systems.

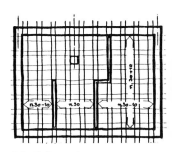

'Ideal' dimensions

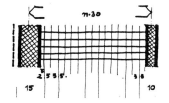

Structural elements: 10, 15, 20 cm and in between

There is a story about a heartless Englishman who set out one day to translate Shakespeare into 'basic English'. To translate a diversity of architecture (ancient or modern) into any existing or currently proposed components system would be an equally misconceived task.

Stages

One can easily list some of the conditions which would allow the current limitations of established conventions and defended territories to be overcome. Here are a few:

● The study of a *modular co-ordination system* both permissive and fertile, of the spaces it will produce, and of a means to describe materials and techniques which is geared less to profit, more to *performance*.

● A sincere statement of *aims and goals* founded on a general study of the way architecture is currently evolving (mental attitude).

● An administrative procedure which provides information about components while at the same time allowing *coexistence* with existing methods.

● The establishment of a catalogue of *recommended* components, open to all producers.

● Live experiments in real situations, directed, controlled, *sanctioned* and published, where priority is given to the architecture and not the means.

As long as we confine our actions strictly to the sphere of construction, we can only perfect details of technique and of the way the work is organised. On the other hand, if the architecture itself comes into question, actions which now seem discordant and energies that are now restrained can get together, becoming co-ordinated, productive. For this to happen architects will be needed, but not the kind who have so long disguised themselves as industrialists or engineers.

6 COMPUTERS

The computer

The construction system adopted for Emerainville was limited to a precisely defined number of elements, while the participation of future inhabitants involved some urgency of timing. Could using a computer help? We had never been too keen on the idea, but since the opportunity had arisen we took it. CAD, CADr, CAM or CAA (Computer Aided Design, Drawing, Manufacture, or Architecture)?

A change takes place which is fascinating to examine in detail: a technique or a tool modifies little by little both the product and the social relationships of those involved in its manufacture. Thus was the Bronze Age eclipsed with the discovery of Iron. The methods of those who organised industry were always reductive and brutal while they were using relatively crude machines. This is clear enough in the furniture industry, which destroyed the rich tradition of timber construction to replace it with chipboard technology: wood ground to a paste, moulded into panels, then covered with a layer of artificial wood grain. Only after this paleo-industrial stage has it been possible to make things which are a little more complicated, but such products are still far from civilised.

We have experienced the same changes in our encounters with the computer. The first program to which we hitched our machine was very basic, it had been designed to turn out a dreadful kind of shoe-box bungalow for African use. We had to unstitch it and knit it together in quite a different way, making it less automatic and more civilised. The 'computerised' architect should surely not be limited to what can be run through his mill!

It is much more complicated to program a number of moves which are simple but varied than to cope with a few complicated moves which are always repeated. This is the difference between mechanism and process, between construction and architecture, between the complicated and the complex. However, the mechanistic view suits contractors and the proponents of those industrial construction systems which go no further than reducing the traditional complexity of the building craft to a few brutal and oppressive gestures. Their computers are programmed to prohibit the degree of differentiation and creativity which the machine makes possible, for they operate only according to the most basic and repetitive procedures. Their usual product might just as well be turned out by a photocopier.

Closed computers

The restrictions on the open-endedness which the computer could allow occur in various ways. For a start there is the question of computer languages, which tend to be self-contained and deliberately incompatible with one another. Already there are several brands and types of instrument with little exchange of information possible between them, while often even hardware from the same firm or software from the same programmer cannot be linked. There are means of translating from one language to another, but this has yet to be fully developed. In addition, the first programs of a few years ago often allowed only one type of building to be drawn, often a deplorable object, though repeated with virtuosity. We have seen programs for setting out drawings so specialised that they could not even follow an oblique line, a curve, or cope with variations in height.

Artificial Intelligence

Some computer enthusiasts approach the subject of CAD more superstitiously than rationally: one always catches the stench of the artificial. Even the label 'Computer Aided Design' is misleading; to call it Computer Use in Design (CUD) would be more appropriate. For it is the architect (among others) who creates and not his pencil: a good pencil can help, but then so can a holiday in the mountains. The term CAD arises out of industrial methodology; here we are again, taking our lead from the mechanics. Architecture is smothered in such a micro-world, fragmented. It can only find its *raison d'etre* in an infinity of interactions which are not always rational. There is nothing to be gained through the use of the random button, for this is only a means of producing a false kind of chance limited by the capabilities of the machine and predictable by another machine of equivalent performance.

We find here again that totalitarian tendency which seeks to dominate the expression of collective, instinctive and emotional attitudes, replacing them with calculated mechanisms (sometimes including a little programmed chance) instead of providing them with a web of possibilities, a fertile ground from which they can grow, finding their own form, using the machine to preserve innate complexities. This fascination with Artificial Intelligence, is it not just another manifestation of something already familiar? In the realm of work we call it Taylorism, in the administrative realm bureaucracy.

Some enthusiasts have become deeply involved in one of these directions and, seduced by the game, have come almost to believe that their creation had taken on a life of its own, like the mythical sculptor who became so engrossed in his paternal fantasy that he asked his carved figure, 'But why don't you speak?' They confuse the infinite diversity of the real world with their stereotyped calculations, which give hard substance to illusions in a world made entirely artificial through careful limitation of parameters. At the same time they call it Artificial Intelligence and sometimes give it the task of conceiving an architecture (or rather the product of a computer game which some persist in calling architecture). Perhaps they will discover the kind of planning which consists of 'containers lined up along the motorway but prettily decorated'? The only ones who really believe in it are the architects who have become spellbound. The computer illusion can be dazzling: architects who see themselves as showmen catch on to it quickly, hoping to raise their rate of production.

Anthropomorphisms

Engineers and contractors, powerful and methodical by nature, have tended to adapt the computer tool to their own image, so much so that they are unable to imagine it otherwise. They add some special features, introduce some variations of appearance, so that 'the architect can play his part'. In their programs however, they reproduce mainly their own hierarchies and compartments: we have seen procedures where sequences allowed no feedback, conceived after the image of the chief designer who passes instructions under his door to the constructor, draughtsman or labourer, idiots by definition.

The computer tool as conceived by industry excludes the architect, but construction by components can allow an architecture which varies in its serial programs; the architect can multiply the number of types while the inhabitant can also vary them. This diversity cannot at present be managed beyond quite crippling limits, but set the computer in the hands of the architect and it could certainly develop.

At present the architect stands alone in his

concern for such diversity, and he sees only too quickly that the whole organisation of 'architecture by components' is in danger of falling prey to additional costs and delays due to diversity, that he is likely to be excluded from the mass production program once again, tolerated as a mere decorator, or restricted to the world of traditional construction. Yet he is really needed for objective reasons: nothing will adequately replace the architect in the building process. Twenty years of dominance by engineers (sometimes with the help of ghost-architects) has made this abundantly clear.

Our research into CAD

In our research into CAD we were obliged first of
all to design in traditional construction and only
later in construction systems. After that we were
finally able to apply it to the organisation of real
components. The instrument has a mania for
precision like an old maid: it can only produce
absolutes, plans ready for immediate execution.
The minimal performance specification for an
architect's program should include the coordination of plans, sections, elevations,
perspectives, measured details, besides the
processing of specifications, estimates and
setting up an information library. To take a
particular example, if we choose a modular coordination system we should be able to start with
interior grids (including breaks) and then fill in the
construction components more or less automatically, each with its own rules of location and
fit, without the instrument preventing us from
indulging in all the exceptions we might desire.
This could prepare the way for an easy transition
from construction systems to a real components
policy.

CAD, CADr, CAM,CAA or CAAs

CAAs – computer Aided Assembly – possibly a
new way of looking at the economy of
construction. A combination of CAD and CAM
(resulting from the use of robots) leads to new
concentrations of power which have to compete
to survive. What will happen to small firms and
self-builders? The computer can help their
professional organisation directly (accounting,
time scheduling are already happening, bit by
bit). They should become more competitive than
the giants, for they can be more flexible. A
program should be able to calculate every aspect
of their work and organise it according to
schedule: they can then concentrate on running

CAD and working relationships
*How would CAD reinforce or
diminish our division of labour?
Would it make some of us
specialists as conceiver-creators,
others as mechanics servicing the
output of the machine and
publishing the documents
(drawings, figures and texts),
destine others still to manage the
operation? We have believed until
now that ways will arise eventually
of vulgarising the machine: less
expensive equipment and less
specialised operations.*

*We have not had to wait for CAD
to see an automatic division of
labour. Some degree of
specialisation is necessary to
guarantee continuity (according to
ability and preference). Nevertheless, we have always tried to
alternate roles, to avoid getting
too type cast, by taking turns (and
following various initiatives). One
person might direct an operation
on one occasion, then find himself
obliged to obey his former
assistant on another.*

*Until now CAD does not seem to
have disrupted the organisation of
labour any more than did the
typewriter or photocopier.
However at present its
manipulation is too specialised for
really general use.*

their sites without losing technicians' time through administrative tasks. Without CAAs the computer is in danger of disrupting such professions in the same way as the introduction of VAT eliminated small shopkeepers who couldn't afford an accountant.

he computer and its use by
rchitects
ievitably the partial automation
f drawing by computer will
eplace draughtsmen already
iade automatic by the boredom
f their work: those old pillars of
ie establishment who work
iechanically, necessarily without
nagination. They face the same
ind of extinction as American
irm workers did, when, during
ie course of a century's
iechanisation, their numbers
iere reduced to one twentieth.
ind even those who escaped are
iot the same . . . this evolution is
iot necessarily pernicious if it is
iot forced. But it is ineffective
ixcept in the short term) to
iarricade oneself behind
igulations, like house painters in
iew York during the Great
iepression who restricted the
ridth of brushes.

In this Malthusian view, some
orporatists are only interested
iat architects should remain
mployed. But draughtsmen,
irveyors and quantity surveyors
iould be equally concerned. They
io should have feared the arrival
f prefabrication which
npoverished construction, as we
iow only too well, and which
xiled designers without replacing
iem, failing to apply similar
conomies to the other
rofessions. It is hardly surprising
iat the prefabricated object
irned out to be sterile:
nproductive of care or
iaintenance, it did not grow
xtensions either.

From theory to practice

We fed our construction system into our computer. This has to be done in two stages. The first involved finding out its physical constraints, especially those which remain implicit: it took us weeks, for example, to find out that the assembly sequence for the building envelope was important only for site work and not for the drawing (the computer is by its nature anti-temporal). The second stage involved incorporating these constraints into the procedures for creating plans. Finally we had to create a library of available components. As soon as our architectural plans are fixed and referenced by hand, we set up a 60 x 60 cm grid (with breaks) within the internal perimeter. We place the bearing walls of various thicknesses and then the partitions. We search in our component library for industrial elements in concrete: first the corners and three dimensional bearing elements, then the standard panels, partitions, floors and their voids.

The external joinery is drawn from the same library and set into the walls. After that the partitions and their doors can be added, then the interior components: stairs, sanitation etc, each time according to another reference in the same library; finally sanitary units, electrical services, plumbing and ventilation can be added.

An alternative program concerns only the perimeter walls, external construction, and designation of entries and exits, creating clusters of dwellings which can be stored in our electronic library. These can then be placed at their respective angles within the general plan whose precise outline and other elements will have been set up by keyboard according to Lambert coordinates.

Unfortunately, until now the necessary computers and their controlling programs have cost more than five times an architect's annual salary. Thus only large offices can afford them and there is a danger that they will gain a monopoly on suitable jobs, ending up desecrating the landscape in the same way as did the prefabricators and manufacturers of endlessly repeated house-types. It is therefore an urgent necessity that instruments and programs be devised which cost much less, and these could be made extendable by module to cope with drawings, accounts or text. Even now a great number of instruments exist which can be connected together in a network without the need for an expensive central unit. The scale of the tools influences the transformation of the landscape very directly, just as it was earlier affected by the arrival of the crane and articulated lorry.

At a more regional scale, the computer can allow a choice of components in real competition with each other or according to some special local arrangement (to help a firm in trouble, for example). Unfortunately the modification of plans and specifications takes months of work, and this can be prohibitive. Even so, it allows real comparison of price and performance between a variety of construction components.

User participation and industry
Having drawn up 30 or so differen
houses for the different families a
Emerainville, we asked our
industrialist how long it would tak
to price them. To do so he would
have to have the plans drawn with
panels and to make calculations;
even with simplified techniques i
takes nearly a day per plan. So we
should have waited a month and
half, and in the meantime the
families would have given up: thi
is how industry prohibits
participation. Unless of course
there is a quick way to set up plans
and cost them: CAD

The evolution of CAD systems

The next stage of evolution, more industrial, which could have developed alongside the previous one, would have been to devise a specialised program according to industry's own ideas of automation. We could have asked the computer to propose its own means of controlling the grids automatically superimposed on architects' plans, taking account of the elements one by one: structure, beams, voids, mezzanines, flues. Next it would determine the priorities: nodes and three-dimensional junctions, floors, bearings and columns, primary and secondary bays, distances covered by the radius of the crane, and finally it would control the production schedule of the factory. Such a total reliance on automation, however, would be both absurd and unhealthy.

Modifications
When the work program of a prefabrication factory is disrupted due to failure or to

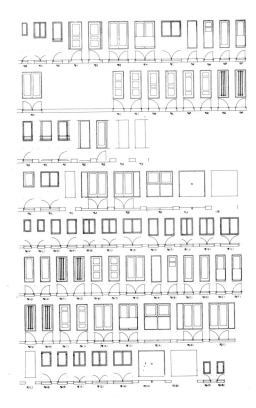

Doors and windows

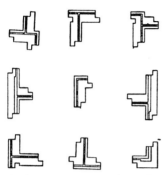

Prefabricated elements (nodes)

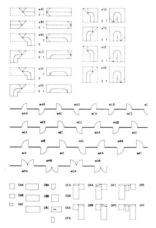

Stairs, doors etc.

commercial or administrative delays, the relevant part of the factory closes down or works at a loss, for the huge investment in design work prohibits changing any element without considerable delays.

Computer-aided *drawing* allows quick changes in coordination for an operation already in motion, so one could take over prefabrication plant made available by a cancelled order or could go to another firm. Every modification of program or schedule tends to consume so much

Classification

The nomenclature of component already implies attitudes of dominance or of coexistence wit the environment: it is by no mean neutral.

It starts with an inclination toward zoning which is already military/ industrial by implication (though pointlessly so). The card index then becomes a symbolic territory to be divided into rational compartments destined to accep all possibilities. We know, though that 'reasonable' human usage will only choose a few of these. This fever for pigeon-holing is reflected in Universal Decimal Classification and in the SfB (already prettier in appearance) which serve to multiply all criteria by all criteria: each criterion takes the place of one case. In contrast with our computer we only use six signs to describe an element (Adam in his earthly paradise was given a whole language with which to name things and had no trouble with logical classification, only with love). Our six cases onl indicate six criteria. And yet we all exhaust ourselves in remorselessly naming simple things according to a complex classification system. Each of our six cases, though, contains two letters and two figures; multiplied by one another they produce a register with millions of places. This should have been sufficient . . . .

Leaving aside such abstractions, let us imagine this register in the form of a landscape made up of our constructions, our sentimental compositions, and let us place in family groups the elements which we use every day, ignoring the whole range of objects possible in the abstract because we would soon be smothered by them. We enter this landscape like villagers carrying with them all their own disorder and individual history. Military minds lose their mathematical approach in such a setting. The individual trees which make up a forest are not significant only by virtue of their position and coordinates in the grid, they find their identity also through their own virtues or in the spirit of the dryad. A few references from the computer library suggest images, associate ideas, provide a basis for local culture and, when used, become obvious. But even with ISO (International Standards Organisation) there are a few codes or graphic symbols which are directly useable.

We have not found any kind of nascent collective tradition which might encourage us to choose a particular vocabulary: all computer systems seem to be culturally and commercially self-contained. It has required considerable effort even to get Anglo-Saxon mechanisms to work with the French language. How can things be named with three letters? We wanted to experiment with our classification system: there was little response.

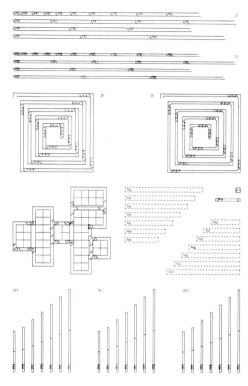

Prefabricated walls

of an architect's energy that changes are often prevented by fear of delays, errors, and confusion. Every modification automatically affects delivery dates, details, and runs back into the working drawings, specifications and estimates or forward into the schedules of manufacturers and contractors. The computer can allow one to take account of the tightest schedules, and thus respond to the changing nature of the economic, social, or geographical context.

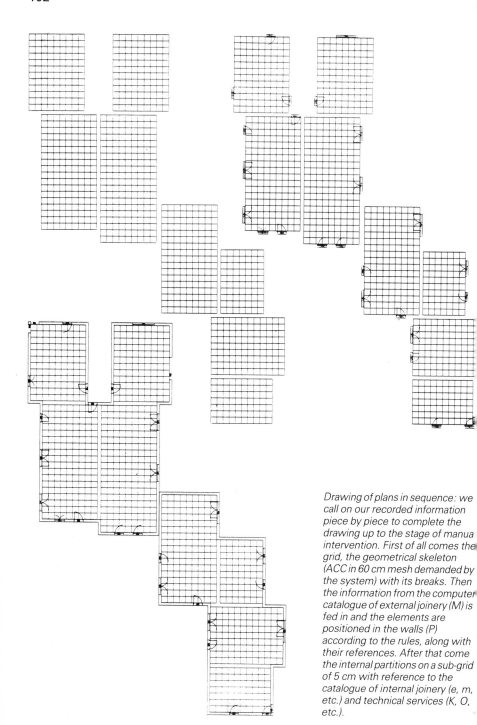

Drawing of plans in sequence: we call on our recorded information piece by piece to complete the drawing up to the stage of manual intervention. First of all comes the grid, the geometrical skeleton (ACC in 60 cm mesh demanded by the system) with its breaks. Then the information from the computer catalogue of external joinery (M) is fed in and the elements are positioned in the walls (P) according to the rules, along with their references. After that come the internal partitions on a sub-grid of 5 cm with reference to the catalogue of internal joinery (e, m, etc.) and technical services (K, O, etc.).

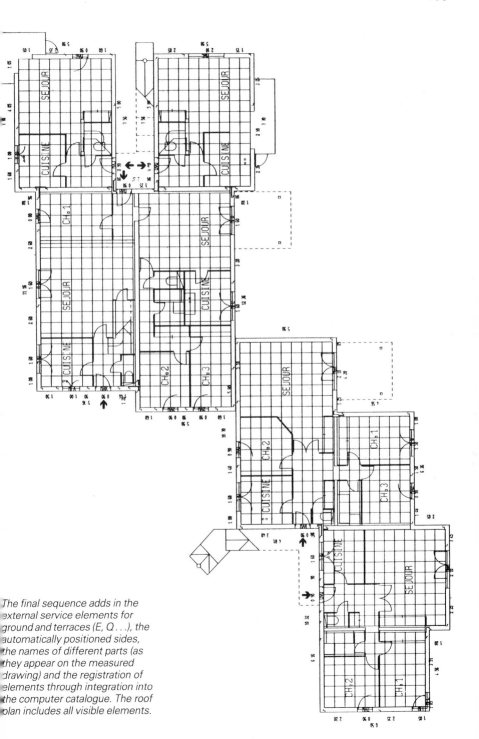

The final sequence adds in the external service elements for ground and terraces (E, Q . . .), the automatically positioned sides, the names of different parts (as they appear on the measured drawing) and the registration of elements through integration into the computer catalogue. The roof plan includes all visible elements.

Facade sequence: the information fed in to produce the plan drawings can determine the elevation outline and positions of windows automatically, and sometimes also the roofs if they are simple. We then add by hand all the superstructure of the facade: it is pointless to process everything through the machine, and there is a danger if we do that laziness will prevent us making full use of our catalogue of elements. The manual drawing is made on top of the computer print by adding the textures of the various kinds of cladding with pencil or self-adhesive sheets, leaving them easy to change without disrupting the rest.

Facade sequence

Estimates

As in preparing a quotation, the quantities are automatic. We began to use a procedure of calculation by ratios which our prefabrication firm had developed with some skill. Once the units had been well defined the price could be worked out automatically.

Power of the tool over the product

The computer has a built-in and cunning tendency to dominate, to reorganise things in its own image (but who made it so?). It only accepts such material as it can digest, lending it in the process an absolute precision, often at a stage where a softer, vaguer approach would be more appropriate. It is logical, certainly, but what if tacit, approximate, irrational aspects were the most vital?

It automates as much as possible and discourages every attempt to differentiate. It loves bureaucratic procedures, making them self-contained and efficient, and it even provides necessary alibis (the computer doesn't make mistakes, etc.). It imposes a homogeneity and allows no form of expression but its own.

How does one resist? First one must remember that the over-precise results are only provisional hypotheses despite their final appearance and one must be determined to disbelieve them. This is only possible through making modification of data as easy as its introduction. One must also dismantle some of the automation, reduce the tendency to run on regardless, and preserve the widest possible choice of menu. This will of course both complicate the program and require more commitment from the architect-operator.

It would be absurd to draw everything on the machine. We must take care not to limit architecture to what can be mechanised and to

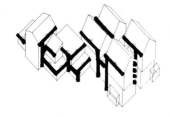

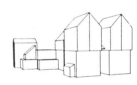

Domesticating the Beast

We have remained resolutely
resistant to computer mythology
resistant to computer mythology
and notions like 'the computer has
decided . . .'. The first of these
myths is already with us; though
crude it has already become
tactical, evolving in three stages:

1 Programs take a long time to
write and are expensive: therefore they must be amortised over
long runs.
2 They economise on manual
work, therefore everything must
be automated.
3 Automation prohibits
differences and exceptions,
therefore one should only allow
those that the computer can put
up with. The rest is then demoted
to marginal status, parked in
'marginal zones'. In precisely the
same way, a few years ago,
nothing could be constructed
which could not be described on
paper, with drawings,
specifications and estimates. Oral
explanation and dialogue was
going to be exceptional from then
on. A good starting point for the
artificial.

Now everyone sincerely believes
that the future of architecture
belongs exclusively to the
computer, and that like the earlier
paper world, it can allow neither
variety nor change. We will come
to regret the passing of the time
when subtleties were allowed, for
this era will soon be eclipsed like
that of stone and the craftsman.

This is certainly wrong, but how
else can one prove it to be so than
by forcing the computer to
produce a varied architecture just
before the producers and
mechanics decide that it is
impossible?

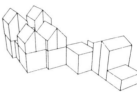

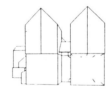

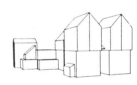

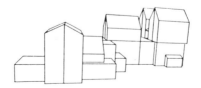

smother it in the process by our misunderstanding. For industrial methodology and the computer threaten to combine in a mood of mutual admiration to plane yet another layer off poor old architecture. Thus by necessity (for our program has not yet evolved far enough to draw everything) and by our own desire to preserve our mental health, we operate both manually and mechanically at the same time. In practice this seems to us more efficient, even when making minor changes.

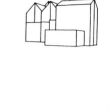

Conception with components

In practice we already used the technique of drawing on several layers of tracing paper superimposed over one another and reproduced together by virtue of their transparency. It could be a somewhat acrobatic working method. A manual base layer was drawn in pencil and this received self-adhesive additions. We tried this kind of duplex drawing for planning studies. It was a slow business because the plan of existing features had to be brought up to date as often as the proposed plan. It was like the old mop with the new head and the new handle. But with the machine, when data change we are not forced to redraw by hand everything that has not been mechanised: the machine tracings serve as a base for the plan and can quite easily be updated.

We should also contrast our operations with work executed on paper, representational, fixed and difficult to update. Plans and elevations need be no more than assembly schemes which show (once only) the position and connections of each element represented by an image, symbol, figure or shape. Each element so marked is referred to a notebook of details, a description, a prototype, or a space left undefined to allow for later development (by the craftsman, the inhabitant etc.). We should then analyse this

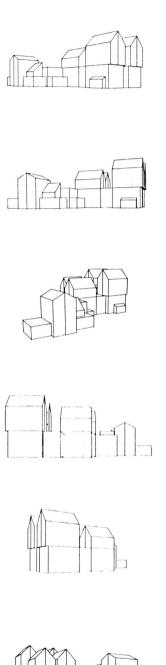

information and rearrange it in stages of increasing precision.

This means of organising our conceptual process sequentially prepared us both for the use of the computer (CAD) and for working with industrial components, without our falling victim to the new tools. These include our libraries of self-adhesive sheets, our modular coordination, our drawings on independent layers, our method of exploratory prototypes, our studies organised in stages of increasing precision with repetition at a local rather than general scale, and above all our varied way of organizing a large number of identical components.

Our way of running-in the drawing with independent layers has helped us to program floor plans into the computer process: every transparent layer that we superimpose on a plan can become a batch of computer information. Our self-adhesive sheets are drawings of prefabricated elements: these have turned into a library of floppy discs. Having simplified and reduced our plans, we used to glue them onto the general plan of site and services: this is now done by computer, but it is essentially the same operation.

Thus, despite two ways of working, the information is only given once (less risk of errors and variations), and the elements are prepared in an autonomous manner (in a provincial factory, for example), but are nonetheless compatible: they fit together neatly into successive sub-groups. Finally our modular coordination procedures easily structure the space to welcome elements which will be compatible with it (or others, with adaptations). For some time already we have been assembling components on paper: now it is only necessary that industry produce some which are really industrial, compatible and civilised.

Transmission of instructions

The cathedrals were built according to instructions transmitted orally with the help of a few sketches in two or three dimensions. The printing press and paper then intervened, and little by little took over the essential part of the task. At the beginning of this century all specific information was contained in one finished drawing in ink with coloured washes; often this covered the specificiation and measurements, and was the sole record for the contract. As far as the general details and construction methods were concerned, the notion of 'the best current practice' carried enough legal weight. Victor Horta could still say 'Do it in the traditional way, my man', and that was enough.

Only later did complications arise. The general technical and administrative clauses became more detailed and were imposed by central authority, often taking no account of local practices and climate. These rules then lost all subtlety of interpretation and became compulsory: with the help of changes in construction they became punitive, bureaucratic shackles. The specifications became longer, the drawings had to be comprehensive, renouncing automatically anything which is difficult to represent through the usual plans and sections (curves and diagonals in space are discouraged). Oral instructions also disappeared along with the old way of describing work by a manual gesture, drawing shapes in the air or on the ground.

Orthogonal projections

The architect's particular schizophrenia comes of having to represent three dimensions in two. To reconstitute an object from a series of plans always requires some effort, so it is tempting to simplify. Unfortunately one then obliges the observer only to understand well that part for

Axonometrics

We have always conceived our architecture through internal and external perspectives, X-ray like and quickly drawn by hand. Only later did we translate these into orthogonal projections, and what they gained in terms of precision they lost in terms of overall legibility. However some information is too fragmented among plans and elevations: we could only coordinate it and explain it to contractors by means of perspectives (and axonometrics for greater precision). This is necessary, for example, to understand the arrangement of rainwater pipes on a building of some complexity, or the changes of cladding from surface to surface and from volume to volume.

We intend to replace elevations by axonometric perspectives in CAD: with views in plan and section the drawn record will be more complete and more explicit. Working directly on perspectives, it should be possible to convey the information automatically back into plans and sections: this development is yet to come.

We take advantage of every means to avoid 'ideal form'. The circumstances of time and place, if one explores them sensitively, suggest subtle variations which rational methods fail utterly to take account of.

However, those usually responsible for conception do their best to eliminate every trace of the 'here and now', categorising all proposed variations according to artificial models, so anxious are they to leave nothing to chance. We are not going to see a relaxation of procedures or a delegation of creative powers overnight.

Before we had our computer, we created a catalogue of self-adhesive sheets depicting all the elements or sub-assemblies which we might use again. We only had to transfer this information into electronic storage; our working methods were already appropriate.

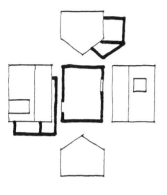

which he is immediately responsible. It may work well enough for the sphere and the shoebox but it is much more difficult to reconstruct the continuity of even a slightly complex architecture. The observer needs to consult at the same time (and take in) at least two plan views, two elevations and two sections.

This method of projection is poor and has few alternatives. We tried turning the facades down onto the plan like the Egyptians; it was mainly our engineers who couldn't follow this convention.

We are repeating the anachronism of harnessing an internal combustion engine between the shafts of a carriage to create a car. Our orthogonal projections date back to a time when descriptive geometry was difficult, but now we have a computer which can instantly resurrect three dimensions!

And the landscape

The computer tool models itself on the interests of those who are charged with organising it. At current prices both hardware and software are beyond the means of all but large offices. Such offices are in danger therefore of monopolising orders once again and of desecrating the landscape in much the same way as the prefabricators and mass bungalow builders have already done. They do not construct the landscape, rather they deconstruct it.

At present a good work station involves rental costs equivalent to employing two architects. It needs to cost far less and thus become available to twenty times as many architects. The hardware always adapts, it is the software which must be changed, mainly to take account of the landscape. Instead of concentrating primarily on matters of technique and economy, in other words of defining the object, the program should concern itself with the existing landscape. It must insert into it the new element and its variants, check their compatibility with the context and then present it visually for the benefit of laymen. It will become a contemporary instrument when it favours the interaction of new partners in the creation of landscape (inhabitants, neighbourhood committees, neighbours, informal groups), whereas without their involvement the landscape will continue to be mechanised.

Table classifying division of work, for technical and administrative purposes

1.	[Preparatory ground works]
1.TRP	Généralités
1.D	Travaux préparatoires
1.B	Terrassements
2.	[Drainage]
2.ASS	Généralités
2.C	Réseaux d'EP
2.U	Réseaux d'EU
2.E	Fossés et plans d'eau
3.	[Structure]
3.STR	Généralités
3.L	Couches de fondations
3.S	Couches de base
4.	[Service networks]
4.RXD	Généralités
4.O	Eau potable
4.G	Gaz
4.J	Electricité
4.X	Eclairage public
4.T	PTT et Télédistribution
5.	[Cladding]
5.RVT	Généralités
5.V	Couches de roulements
5.b	Bordures, bordurettes, etc
6.	[Planting]
6.PLT	Généralités
6.Z	Engazonnements
6.A	Arbres
6.a	Arbustes
6.H	Haies
6.m	Plantes grimpantes
6.s	Plantes tapissantes
6.n	Plantes aquatiques
7.	[Street furniture]
7.MOB	Généralités
7.W	Composants en bois
7.F	Composants en métal
7.K	Jeux
7.P	Signalisation
7.Q	Divers

1.	[Infrastructure]
1.INF	Généralités
1.B	Terrassements
1.L	Fondations
1.U.	Sous-sols
1.G	Rez
1.r	Réseaux incorporés
2.	[Structure]
2.STR	Généralités
2.P	Eléments de structure(s)
2.M	Menuiseries extérieures
2.E	Escaliers extérieurs
2.W	Charpente
2.H	Lanterneaux
3.	[Envelope]
3.VET	Généralités
3.Z	Zinguerie
3.T	Couvertures
3.V	Enduits, bardages, etc
3.t	Terrasses
4.	[Partitions]
4.PAR	Généralités
4.e	Escaliers intérieurs
4.p	Cloisonnement
4.m	Menuiseries intérieures
4.v	Revêtements intérieurs
4.f	Serrurerie
5.	[Services]
5.EQU	Généralités
5.J	Electricité
5.K	Chauffage
5.O	Plomberie
5.R	Ventilation
6.	[Superstructure]
6.SUP	Généralités
6.F	Serrurerie
6.Q	Garde-corps, pergolas,etc
7.	[Finishes]
7.FIN	Généralités
7.C	Peintures extérieures
7.c	Peintures intérieures
7.s	Revêtements de sol

Only after such tentative progress will the computer move on to facilitate calculated construction and its details, organise their breakdown into industrial products and allow a choice of elements by the new partners in the generative process.

The capacity of tools influences the landscape quite directly: the crane and the articulated lorry have already made their mark.

Uzès, France

7 A GENERAL VIEW

Modular coordination
We have experimented practically for many years with methods of construction in several countries, always on the lookout for evidence about the use of modular grids, and we present our arguments below in order of importance.

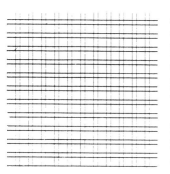

A preamble
Our desire for theoretical perfection sometimes leads to ideal solutions which are impracticable or purely decorative. They follow the image of perfect coordination slavishly, which demands that all technical dimensions conform to the module precisely, but this can only be achieved in practice by blowing up or planing down the industrial elements to an inappropriate degree. If one can reasonably force elements longer than one metre to the nearest dimension divisible by 10 cm, they will not tend to fit a system based on multiples of 30 cm. Similarly one cannot simply thicken a 15 cm element to 20 cm for the sake of the module. In our Medical Faculty buildings columns were often 20 cm thick, but this was a special case. A bathroom which happened to be 2.75 metres long can quite easily be reduced to 2.70 metres, for this is a change of less than 5%. The 10 cm grid works well enough, while the 30 cm is out of proportion because it demands more than 10% adjustment. The precise percentage depends on materials, techniques, rules of construction and local practices. A wall can be changed from 15 cm to 16 easily enough (4%) but not from 15 cm to 20 cm (25 or 33%). One could set up a standardisation of partition walls on increments of 2.5 cm with 5 cm preferred: 10, (12.5), 15 (17.5), 20 (22.5), 25 cm. (Even better would be a duodecimal system: 12 18, 24 cm on a grid of 12 + 24 = 36 cm).

Manufacturers do not bother very much about modular coordination any more: they just follow calculations and established standards. Even so, it would be necessary to readjust either the techniques or the rules to achieve truly

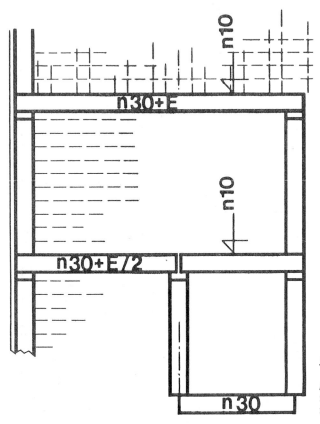

SAR section

Levels are standardised from floor to floor, and an adaptor takes up the difference.

standardised dimensions. For a long time already, we have been using elements in all sizes, and perhaps this represents a richness worth preserving. This is another example of the temptation to limit the sizes of products too strictly; to give too much power to a modular system instead of expecting it simply to help a large number of products varied in origin or

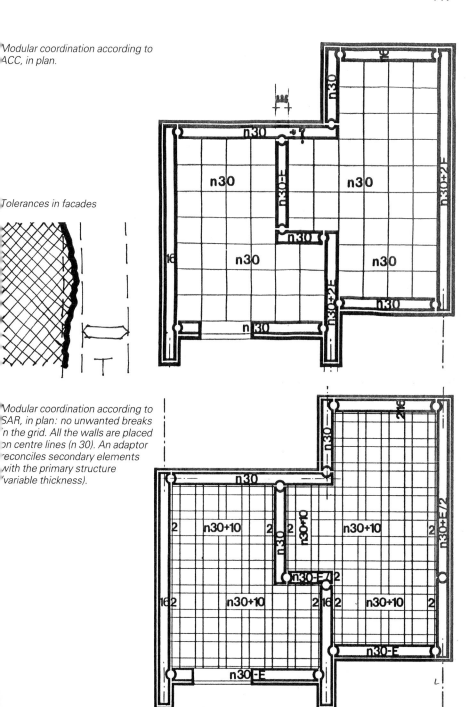

Modular coordination according to
ACC, in plan.

Tolerances in facades

Modular coordination according to
SAR, in plan: no unwanted breaks
in the grid. All the walls are placed
on centre lines (n 30). An adaptor
reconciles secondary elements
with the primary structure
(variable thickness).

purpose to fit together without destroying their differences. We must not standardise construction elements any more forcefully than the buildings they contribute to or the dwellings within: it is all part of the same attitude. It would be better delicately to manage the inevitable diversity of technical dimensions (remeasuring them carefully) than to impose a brutal conformity. The modular grid should allow several levels of intervention. If m = 10 cm, for example, one might need 3m, $^m/_2$, $^m/_4$ depending on the precision and scale of each element.

When facades get thinner towards the top, and if it is necessary to keep the external surface bare and continuous, the wall elements become displaced from their centre line and by virtue of their different thicknesses leave increasing spaces internally. These differences are taken up at the corners by returns which are poured in situ or prefabricated onto the corner elements. Alternatively they can be displaced sideways while the next joint along is enlarged. Floors follow this displacement.

First argument
The axes of bearing elements should always be based on multiples of 3m, whatever the thicknesses of the elements themselves. This controls the placing of all primary structure (and should apply to secondary elements too) while it prevents departures from the grid and the faking-up consequent to such disturbances. It seems illogical to disrupt the placing of primary elements for the sake of allowing regularity in secondary ones: this is what happens in the ACC system with bearing walls set to one side of the 30 cm grid lines. The secondary elements are always upset by uncontrollable breaks with the grid, merely for the sake of incorporating elements whose conformity to multiples of 30 cm remains pointless.

Adaptation

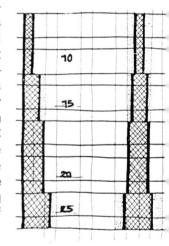

Extra long prefabricated panel, or increased width of joint

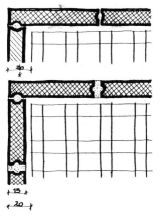

Second argument

Thicknesses. The bearing walls for most dwellings are between 10 cm and 20 cm thick (so the SAR system which standardises them at 10 cm grid space is problematic). We place them firmly on the axis of the 20 cm grid space and the distance between wall surface and grid line becomes a haphazard *zone of adjustment.* This practice is logical, straightforward, and links us directly with an evolving tradition.

Our zone of adjustment allows us to set up an interior grid (always less than 10 cm). It allows wall thicknesses independence of the grid, so one can adjust them without disrupting internal planning. This is useful if one needs to change from one product to another in the course of design or on site, or if the walls change thickness from floor to floor.

Third argument

Lack of sophistication. We must envisage stringent economic limits, and consequently little perfection of appearance. Externally applied insulation makes the expensive virtuosity of panel systems with built-in insulation unnecessary, and in any case these have hardly proved satisfactory or weather-proof. If the insulation covers everything, the basic wall can be left rough.

Fourth argument

The external and internal walls can be left identical. However, the edges of floor elements will differ depending on whether one or two edges are placed on an external or internal wall, and depending on the displacement of walls to be placed on top.

Fifth argument

Heterogeneous construction. Concrete need only be used where it is really necessary. It should be relieved where possible by frequent transitions to other materials which are more suitable: this will be less dull and more economical. In addition the composition of concrete can vary, as can its thickness according to its use, position, the locality, etc.

We propose heterogeneous construction: heavy panels can alternate with partitions that are lighter, more diverse and above all modifiable by the inhabitants themselves (timber or metal, for example). Each system of construction has its own assembly method and its own expression. It would be unhealthy to do everything with the same material: this would be a denial of the compatibility of components. At the same time the site must be organised to allow jobs to take place sequentially in a harmonious manner.

For example, 30 cm solid wall elements cast in lightweight concrete, then clad and plastered, provide envelope and insulation at the same time. It is possible to use this for very large lightweight panels. There are many similar possibilities.

Sixth argument

The joints. Wall elements cannot exceed the modular grid. The fixing grooves of the element's edges may be filled in, for example, with an expanding plastic mortar pumped in from bottom to top. The joints are filled with mastic or well positioned to be covered up by other elements. They require a genuine dry assembly, welded or bolted.

Seventh argument
In section storey heights are standardised, and not the height between floors. This standardises elements which run from floor to floor: external cladding, service pipes etc. Floors are also regulated by the 10 cm module. It must be possible to vary floor heights according to region, use, local conditions, peoples' wishes etc.

Combined research
We are now involved in a program of research into, and experiment with, a process which combines industrial components with the work of craftsmen to produce an organic architecture. This research runs parallel with real projects, which can serve both as a demonstration and as a continuing stimulus. We are aiming for a more realistic industrialisation of building, concentrating also on attitudes and techniques. The practical experiment will consist of a series of self-controlled sequences entrusted to a group of contractors. It will be organised according to simple geometries and assembly methods which can be constructed in any kind of architecture accepting any kind of component.

In current circumstances it would be illogical to favour one more super-system of construction which might turn out to be just as limited as those that have gone before: far better to make a 'giant concrete block' in all sizes with holes in any position, very cheap and available to all small firms. It should not be assembled by the manufacturer: firms are less 'industrial' when they want to take over the whole process of construction.

The geometry of components should be based on a finer modular system to determine lengths, widths, thicknesses, densities, positions of holes, connections with identical elements, with components of a different kind, and with the work of craftsmen. The tools should be adapted to ensure diversity yet take due note of economic constraints. This diversity could easily be achieved with computers: CAD could lead in turn to CAM (Manufacture) and computerised control of orders, or CAAs (Assembly) which will automatically produce the working drawings, specifications and estimates.

A tighter modular coordination (leading both to increased rigour and increased diversity) associated with CAD will allow very quick comparison between similar systems and with traditional construction (without the need to modify plans): it can bring a new basis for competition.

Diversity

At the same time we want to test other industrialised components – structures, mechanical services or cladding – and help adapt them to our project. Generally speaking, from the start of our studies we sought to encourage a kind of cross-fertilisation of all lines of research which could contribute to the debate concerning what makes a landscape, a piece of urban fabric, rather than a collection of objects – even well-designed objects. A diverse selection of programs and spatial organisations (town houses, clusters, maisonettes, uses other than residential, etc.) could be projected after a few sessions of participation and consultation with possible inhabitants and users: we know from experience that such participation leads directly to a diversity of arrangements and materials, and brings out considerable concern with public spaces and above all with the road networks. Public and private planting is also an essential component in preserving the continuity of the landscape.

In a few especially spectacular areas, the work of craftsmen will show the way in which the manual and the mechanical can be combined, each in its own sequence with its own expression. Subtle differences will make each building or each dwelling individually recognisable, particularly in the case of the doorways, as the most sensitive point of transition between public and private realms.

These different lines of research will be integrated into a more general movement, each finding its place and justification. Energy saving measures are easily implemented thanks to external insulation, and can be perfected through solar panels, heat pumps, glasshouses etc.

We propose claddings of a more industrial, more economic kind. Their relative crudeness can be relieved with some architectural games. Also there can be 'vegetable cladding': climbing plants add insulation, weather protection and a natural presence.

Preliminary participative consultation and later contacts prepare the inhabitants to put down roots more easily, to get to know each other and to discover how to act together upon their environment. In view of this we take the trouble to leave space for future extensions and to organise the rules of the architecture (both constructionally and culturally) to encourage such initiative. It is as much the readiness to believe as the readiness to get involved which allows a neighbourhood to regenerate itself by itself, and to develop quickly into a vital urban organ.

Et cetera

All this is still being explored, and will be described at a later date.

·